Henry Ford
and the
Jews

HENRY FORD
AND THE
JEWS

ALBERT LEE

STEIN AND DAY /*Publishers*/New York

Library of Congress Cataloging in Publication Data
Lee, Albert, 1942-
  Henry Ford and the Jews.

  Includes bibliographical references and index.
  1. Antisemitism—United States. 2. Ford, Henry, 1863-1947.
3. Jews in the United States—Politics and government. 4. United
States—Ethnic relations.
I. Title.
DS146.U6L43   305.8′924″073   79-3694
ISBN   0-8128-2701-5

To
Carol Allman Lee

CONTENTS

ACKNOWLEDGMENTS

Special appreciation goes to the staffs of two fine organizations: The Ford Archives, Henry Ford Museum, Dearborn, Michigan; and the American Jewish Archives, Cincinnati, Ohio.

Also, I am personally grateful to Philip Slomovitz, Detroit's senior Jewish journalist, who contributed his half-century of personal experience; to Jerry Sloan, of Ford Motor Company Public Relations, who handled my difficult inquiries with a high level of professionalism; and especially to Benton Arnovitz, Executive Editor of Stein and Day, whose knowledgeable and perceptive editing vastly improved this book.

Other resource centers deserve credit, including the Michigan Historical Library, Ann Arbor; the Burton Historical Collection, Detroit; the Walter Reuther Library, Detroit; and, of course, the Library of Congress in Washington, D.C.

Introduction

•

We cannot, by definition, understand Auschwitz, says Elie
Wiesel. Perhaps he is right. The extermination camps of
Auschwitz, Bergen-Belsen, Buchenwald, and Dachau evoke too
heinous an image to gaze upon long for fear our own sense of
security and humanity may be scarred by the vision. Auschwitz,
by definition, is not to be understood. Yet we must. Even though
the notion is now cliché, those who ignore history may be
doomed to repeat it. We must learn what we can of Auschwitz, of
the events and the men who made it inevitable.

One such man who helped pave the road to Auschwitz was an
American. He is remembered today as one of the greatest industrialists of all time, as the man who brought the freedom of
personal transportation and the dignity of a living wage to the
common worker. He is eulogized, schools and streets are named
after him, and a U.S. postage stamp bears his likeness. He is
Henry Ford.

Ford's contribution to international anti-Semitism and the rise of Nazism has never been fully explored. Many have heard that he was anti-Semitic, and pass it off as an eccentricity of an otherwise great man. It deserves far more consideration. Ford's anti-Semitism—which spanned a quarter of a century—influenced, perhaps more than that of any other American, the rise of "racial" hatred toward the Jewish people both on this continent and in pre-Hitler Germany. He used his wealth and heroic stature to inspire an anti-Semitic movement which grew steadily from his first attack on the Jews in 1920 to the outbreak of World War II and beyond. He was the man whom Adolf Hitler had good reason to call "my inspiration."

I began this book ten years ago when I was a writer for Ford Motor Company publications. In that capacity, I traveled to most of the Ford plants and facilities in thirty-nine states. I had occasion to talk frequently with Ford old-timers while doing human-interest articles for the corporation's employee newspaper and magazine. The tales I heard about Henry Ford's attitude toward the Jews were, frankly, unbelievable to me then. So I began to investigate, digging as far as I could into not only what Ford did, but why. Was it the influence of other suspected anti-Semites, including Thomas Edison and Ernest Liebold, who set him on his campaign against the Jews, or the episode of Ford's ill-fated Peace Ship during World War I, or some much broader combination of social and personal influences? We will investigate all of these possibilities and more in the final chapter. Once I felt I understood Henry Ford's motivation, a revelation which has occurred only recently, I felt ready to tell his story.

But at the outset, I would like to place this book in historical perspective. While it is true that the anti-Semitic materials developed by Ford are still popping up in American neo-Nazi propaganda and in European and Arab countries, it is equally true that the Ford Motor Company today is entirely blameless. As Philip Slomovitz, the dauntless editor of the *Detroit Jewish News* for more than forty years, puts it: "Henry Ford II has spent most of his life atoning for his grandfather's sins against the Jews." Henry Ford II has been a major contributor to the United Jewish Appeal, the Israel Emergency Fund, the Jewish Welfare Federation, and the Anti-Defamation League of B'nai B'rith, the organization which fought so valiantly against his grandfather. Henry Ford II also established a Ford assembly plant in Israel and has steadfastly kept it in operation, even though it has meant a boycott of all Ford products in Egypt, Syria, Lebanon, Iraq, and Saudi Arabia. In recent months I have carefully scrutinized the operations and management policies of Ford Motor Company for any remnants of Henry Ford Senior's legacy of hatred. I have found none, and would hope that the sins of the grandfather revealed in this book are not visited upon the grandson nor upon the company which bears the family name and which employs 230,000 people.

Rather, this book can serve to more honestly define Henry Ford's place in the history of this century. It is an object lesson in misdirected power and the all-too-common error of allowing knowledge in one area to lend credibility in another. Perhaps most important, this book may serve as another reminder of an era of the most heinous crime in recorded history. If we cannot understand Auschwitz, we must at least never forget the lesson of its causes and consequences.

One question is inevitable. The answer is that I was born an Irish Catholic and am now a Unitarian.

Henry Ford
and the
Jews

1

An American Folk Hero

•

No opponent more formidable than Henry Ford could have existed in the spring of 1920. He was far more than a wealthy industrialist. He was a legend in his own time, a man so admired that his reputation was ranked with that of the immortals. He was decorated by governments around the globe and showered with honorary doctorates, even named as a candidate for the Nobel Peace Prize. A survey of college students rated him as the third greatest man of all time—just below Napoleon and Jesus Christ. A *New York Times* survey of national opinion rated Henry Ford among the top eight Americans who ever lived.[1] As one biographer witnessed, hero worship of Henry Ford was more than an obsession, it was "a canonization creating a Zeus of American mythology."[2]

Ford's wealth was awe-inspiring. He was by far the richest man in the world, with incalculable assets that could only be estimated at well over a billion dollars. In 1914 he took his only son Edsel down to the vaults to show the young man his twenty-first birthday present: $1 million in gold.[3] By the beginning of 1920, Ford was the sole proprietor of the largest industrial empire that had ever been built. He not only produced more than 86,000 cars a month, about 60 percent of the American car market, he retained vast holdings in a wide range of industries, from airplane manufacturing to wood-alcohol distillation.[4] His immense wealth was all the more formidable because he had shown, and would soon prove again in his attacks on American Jews, that he was willing to spend millions to achieve his ends.

But Henry Ford's greatest asset was his personal reputation as a man of the people. His fame was first spread by the machine that he built, the Model T. It was the first automobile which bore a price within reach of the average American family. Henry Ford continued to lower the car's price, from $590 to $525, to $500, and finally all the way down to $260 in 1925. The age of the Tin Lizzie, as the car was called, lasted from October 1908 through May 1927, and in that time more than 15 million Model T's were sold. This was the first car that most Americans had ever seen, the one that freed them from the isolation of rural life; and the man who produced such a vehicle naturally accrued universal gratitude.

In 1914, Ford captured the imagination of the entire world by matching low prices with high wages. Even the lowliest sweeper in his plants would henceforth receive a minimum wage of five dollars a day, an unheard-of amount, considering that the average wage then was twenty-two cents an hour for assemblers. He even shared his profits with all employees, in 1914 distributing approximately $12 million. The press literally exploded with news about the great humanitarian Henry Ford, and accolades came in from every direction, including government, foreign

4

officials, university presidents, and labor leaders. From the
moment of the five-dollar day on, everything Mr. Ford had to say
became headline news.[5]

And Ford had a lot to say He was a relentless and untiring
self-advertiser, believing firmly that mere mention on the front
page was far greater exposure for his company than full-page ads
inside. He was the first industrial leader to prove the value of
public relations. Yet those who knew him well also knew his
vanity. "He went on the theory of keeping the name Ford before
the public," his personal secretary wrote, "not particularly as an
advertising factor so much as a means of upholding his
popularity."[6]

The image Ford projected for himself was that of a modest
farmer who built cars not for profit, but to serve the needs of an
ever-increasing number of people while creating more and better
jobs. He believed in sharing knowledge, as witnessed by his
company policy of making Ford patents free to anyone. He
abhorred monopolies, which he proved in his daring fight
against the Selden patent. George Selden obtained a patent on
the first American auto engine in 1879 and, without ever actually
building a car, was able to keep the patent alive and force all auto
makers from 1911 on to pay royalties to him for every vehicle
sold. Ford refused to pay, eventually beating Selden in court and
freeing the engine design for anyone's use. In the public press
and the boardrooms of competitive auto companies, Ford was
praised as the emancipator of the entire industry.

Ford believed in the social responsibility of management to its
employees and established a social department which cared for
the needs of individual families. He projected an equal employment policy in the laboring ranks, hiring disabled people,
including the blind, and opening the doors to both blacks and
Jews for factory jobs. He had a far-reaching concept of village

5

industries in which the individual worker could live in a small agrarian community, enjoying the benefits of the land, yet work in a community factory, gaining the higher living standard of urban workers. Ford not only advocated such a suburban community, but proposed to build one seventy-five miles long in Alabama by buying up the then incomplete series of dams that would eventually become the Tennessee Valley Authority.

In his private life, Ford appeared to epitomize the humble American laborer. He got up each morning at six and went to work just like any other Ford employee. He believed absolutely in the purity of work, claiming in his biography that "the natural thing to do is to work—to recognize that prosperity and happiness can be obtained only through honest effort."[7] At fifty-seven years old, he lived a simple life, dressing modestly, avoiding any implication of high society, and preferring the company of his wife and twenty-seven-year-old son Edsel, who had naturally come into his father's business. He insisted on absolute cleanliness throughout his plants. He neither smoked nor drank liquor, never serving anything stronger than grape juice to visitors at his Fair Lane estate. He carried on a full-scale war against tobacco, holding that if you "study the history of almost any criminal, you'll find an inveterate cigarette smoker." And he was a dramatic prohibitionist, vehemently declaring that "brains and booze will not mix."[8] He gave his sales department fits by taking such strong positions, even though it meant lost sales to people in the tobacco belt of Virginia and that no Ford trucks would be seen in Milwaukee breweries.[9]

Yet Ford seemed ready to lose sales in many areas in order to play directly to his one primary audience—the American farmer. Here his identification approached absolute reverence. He was, after all, simply a farm boy from a small Michigan community. Like most farmers of the day, he projected a clear distaste and

6

distrust of intellectuals, believing that "too much reading messes up my mind." This conformed well to the rural thinking that excessive intellectual endeavors "made men impotent and women sexless, while men of ideas became bookish, nearsighted sticks."[10] One acquaintance observed that "the only letters he [Ford] takes time to write with his own hand are to little boy and girl friends who are having a birthday."[11] And he played heavily on the agrarian mistrust of middlemen and bankers, looked on with suspicion by American farmers since the mid-nineteenth century. Ford apparently sincerely distrusted bankers and Wall Street business people intensely, avoiding any borrowing, even at the risk of courting financial disaster, and never issuing stock once he had bought out all of his initial backers. His 1922 autobiography, *My Life and Work,* leaves no doubt: "I determined absolutely that never would I join a company in which finance came before the work or in which bankers or financiers had a part."[12] And true to his farm image, he had no respect for city slickers, no matter what their profession: "The modern city is a mistake," he said. "It is overdone. It does not produce the best or the most necessary things. It takes people away from the land. I want to see the day when the country will assume the ascendancy over the city in the affairs of men."[13]

Henry Ford was a gentle man who shared a love of all living things with the naturalist John Burroughs and who shared campfires with his friend Thomas Edison. Ford was known to "nail up a door for a whole season rather than disturb a robin's nest," and he "postponed the hay harvest because ground birds were brooding in the field."[14] He was a man of peace, saying a few years earlier that he would give his entire fortune if he could shorten the Great War (World War I) by a single day.[15]

Here, then, is the wholesome Henry Ford, projecting the image of the All-American boy who made good. It is difficult

7

today to imagine just how large a shadow he cast across the continent in 1920, how earnestly rural people clung to his every word. An indication may be found in a survey done by *Collier's Weekly* in July 1923, which showed Henry Ford defeating President Warren G. Harding by a straw-poll vote of 88,865 to 51,000—and that was after Ford's first major volley of anti-Semitism.

The legend of Henry Ford was largely his own creation. He carefully fostered his image through newspaper and magazine interviews with his favored press people, some of whom went on to write aggrandizing biographies of their benefactor. To the public, Ford was a retiring man who shunned publicity, refused to appear before crowds, and never made speeches. The fact is that Ford obtained publicity on his own terms to best present his own vision. That much of his image was untrue is now a matter of history. Ford, for example, told of his youth on the farm in which a harsh father kept him working in the fields and forbade him to repair watches for neighbors and otherwise develop his mechanical genius. He told how he would wait for his father to go to sleep, then sneak out of the house to find watches and clocks to repair. He worked, Henry said, on a little bench he had constructed in his bedroom with tools he had fashioned in secret. Later he said his father discouraged him from leaving the farm to learn a mechanical trade in the city, and when Ford built his first automobile and brought it home to his father, the uncompromising old man refused to ride in it.[16]

Of these tales of tremendous hardship, his sister Margaret said, there was "no truth in them." Henry's father, William, never discouraged his son from developing his skills. Ford Senior, in fact, maintained a thoroughly equipped tool shop on the farm and the younger Ford had the complete run of it. William got his son his first job in the city, and also spoke with pride of Henry's mechanical skills.[17]

Neither was Henry a true mechanical genius nor a genuine inventor of the automobile. His first car was built primarily through the skills of fellow workers at the Edison Company in Detroit, where Henry worked. He talked thoroughly talented men, including Oliver Barthel, George Cato, Jim Bishop, and Ed Huff, into doing the actual work, while he spent much of his time kibitzing or playing practical jokes, such as nailing one of his comrade's shoes to the floor. Never in his career would Henry Ford actually build a car. As Barthel later said, "I never knew Henry Ford to design a car. I don't think he could. Mr. Ford had no drafting experience at all. He even had difficulty reading a blueprint."[18] But because of his early quadracycle, Ford was able to obtain backers in two early automobile-manufacturing ventures, both of which failed because Ford, according to his most conscientious biographer, Allan Nevins, "sloughed off all responsibility." His third car-building venture, Ford Manufacturing Company, succeeded largely because of the organizational genius of his partner, James Couzens, and the engine, frame, and running gear from John and Horace Dodge.

Perhaps one of the most revealing stories of Henry Ford's ability to manipulate publicity to his advantage is that of how he obtained control of his company. The achievement was all the more remarkable since Ford never invested a nickel for initial stock. The Dodge Brothers sued Henry Ford for withholding profits from shareholders. The judge, and later the state superior court, agreed with the Dodge brothers and ordered Ford to pay the dividends. A few weeks later, Ford held a press conference and stated flatly that he was going to organize a new company, Henry Ford & Son, and sell cars for $250. He would use his share of the dividends, some $12 million, to finance the venture. And, as for the company of which he was now a part: "Why, I don't know exactly what will become of that." It was, of course, all a bluff. Ford had not, in fact, designed a new and cheaper car. But it worked to panic his stockholders. Henry Ford offered to buy out the 41.5 percent of the stock they owned, and if they didn't sell it all to him, he would buy none of it, allowing the company to go under without his name or reputation. The scheme worked. Henry bought up every share of stock.[19]

Sticking to the truth was never a characteristic to which Henry Ford aspired. As William Richards observed in *The Last Billionaire*, "It was less important that a thing be true than that it be exciting, stunning."[20] Ford would make a wild statement to see how it affected the listener and, if it stirred him, Ford would allow the comment to stand. Just one anecdote will show how he was a master at turning any event into good press. On one birthday he put on one old shoe and one new one by mistake while dressing in the dark. When a newsman asked him about it, he said that it was a tradition. Every birthday, he avowed, he put on one old shoe to remind himself that he had been poor. It made excellent copy.

Even Ford's quick wit, however, could not compensate for his lack of education. He believed, for instance, that sugar was harmful because it was a crystal and the sharp edges of the sugar crystal would cut you on the inside. When one of Ford's chemists demonstrated to him that sugar dissolves in water, Henry didn't speak to him for weeks afterward.[21] In another instance, he released the statement that he had voted for the first time for President Garfield in 1884.[22] Someone soon pointed out that Garfield had been assassinated in 1881. The greatest exposure of Ford's shortcomings came when the *Chicago Tribune* accused Ford of being an "ignorant idealist," stating that "the man is so incapable of thought that he cannot see the ignominy of his own performance." Ford sued for $1 million. The case, heard in Mt. Clemens, Michigan, became a public exhibition of Ford's ignorance. The *Chicago Tribune*'s attorney asked if he knew anything about an American Revolution, to which Ford answered, "I understand there was one in 1812." How about the one in 1776? "I didn't pay much attention to such things." He defined the word *ballyhoo* as a "blackguard, I guess." And who was Benedict Arnold? "A writer," he guessed. In the end, Henry won the lawsuit, but, instead of his being awarded $1 million, the judge gave him precisely six cents in damages. The *Chicago Tribune* case embittered Ford against the press and the folly of making public appearances, reaffirming his successful approach of controlling news on his own terms.[23]

The real Henry Ford was also unyielding. "I have never known him to change his mind on any important matter," his biographer and friend Samuel Marquis testified.[24] He was a man who, once setting his sights on an objective or an idea, would not let go. Ford, for example, ran for the U.S. Senate in 1918. It was an absurd campaign, since Ford refused to make a single public appearance or debate any issues with his opponent, Truman Newberry. Ford lost the race, but only by a slight margin. Instead of admitting that he had been outcampaigned— Newberry actually spoke in public—Ford demanded a recount. And when that failed to obtain the desired result. he set out to destroy Newberry and all of his political cronies. Ford and his good friend Harvey Firestone hired 100 private detectives for the purpose. Edwin Pipp, the Dearborn Independent's first editor, recalled that the detectives "began to trip over one another." Ford filed charges with the Department of Justice to stop Newberry from being seated and, when that didn't work, he turned on Senator Townsend of Michigan, who had defended Newberry.

After spending what Townsend called "a steady stream of gold," Ford finally managed to get the Department of Justice to file charges of violation of the Corrupt Practices Act against Newberry and 134 others. He claimed that Newberry had spent more than the law allowed on the campaign. Eventually, Newberry was convicted and resigned his Senate seat for fear of expulsion. Newberry made it clear that he was leaving because of "political persecution" and for the good of his fellow Republicans. Taking his leave, he claimed that "hundreds of agents had hounded and terrified [his supporters] in all parts of the state." In the end, Henry Ford appeared vindicated, since he had not been beaten in a fair contest and had "exposed corruption" in government.[25]

In the spring of 1920, Henry Ford was more than a redoubtable opponent for any group, he was a force far larger than life. Despite his obvious lack of education, he was widely perceived as a genius. He had fostered the myth of his own greatness; now he believed it himself. If he failed, it was clearly the work of some plotters, some sinister force; for he was convinced that Henry Ford was above error. And with the largest accumulation of wealth on earth, he could prove any opponent wrong. Years later, John Kenneth Galbraith correctly took Henry Ford's measure: "Success had made him immune to counsel and advice; for too long he had seen eccentricity and even mere foolishness pictured as genius and had believed it."[26]

2

The Truth According to Ford
•

In announcing the onset of his public attack on the Jews, Ford characteristically began with a private interview by a prominent newsman, J. J. O'Neil of the *New York World*. He told O'Neil he was going to speak out on the neglected truth. "International financiers are behind all war," Ford said. "They are what is called the international Jew: German Jews, French Jews, English Jews, American Jews. I believe that in all those countries except our own the Jewish financier is supreme . . . here the Jew is a threat."[1]

The public announcement was not altogether unexpected by those who knew Ford intimately. For several months prior he had been testing out his biases in personal conversations to get reactions. On a camping trip the previous summer with his good friends Thomas Edison, Harvey Firestone, and naturalist John Burroughs, Ford spoke at great length against the "Jewish capitalists," blaming them for causing the recent world war, for all the "thieving and robbery" in America, and even for the failures of the U.S. navy.[2] On another occasion with one of his senior executives, Ford bit into a candy bar and said it was not as good as it once had been because "the Jews have taken hold of it. They've cheapened it to make more money."[3]

The *New York World* article, however, was the first open shot at the Jews, soon to be followed by the greatest barrage of anti-Semitism in American history. In the spring of 1920 Ford set his personal newspaper, *The Dearborn Independent,* to the task of chronicling the Jewish menace. Every week, for the next ninety-one issues, the paper carried a major story exposing what it defined as some Jewish-inspired evil. The magazine had a circulation of between a quarter and a half million during that nearly two-year period. The most aggressive of these anti-Semitic articles were then reprinted by Ford in four volumes called the *International Jew.* Reprints in quantities of 200,000 each were frequent, and an estimated 10 million copies of the collected anti-Semitic articles were sold in America.[4] The *International Jew* was also translated into sixteen languages, including Arabic. Sales of the *International Jew,* with Henry Ford named on most copies as author, were distributed by the millions in Europe, South America, and the Middle East.[5] Few books have ever gained such wide circulation. Ford's publishing venture was not to make a profit. His magazine solicited and contained no advertising; Ford would not have it subject to any Jewish influence. It sold for five cents a copy, or one dollar a year, and volumes of the *International Jew,* each 225 pages long, sold for just twenty-five cents each. In all, Ford's publishing venture incurred a $4,795,000 loss during its eight-year existence, much of that cost accruing, of course, to the anti-Semitic campaign.[6]

The articles began with the theme of a worldwide conspiracy by Jewish supercapitalists. The Jews were the only and original international capitalists, the pieces maintained. They invented the stock market and the gold standard—all to corrupt and subjugate the "gentile boobs." Capitalists were the world's enemies, and they were always either Jews or "Jewish fronts"— gentiles whom the Jews could control from the background. Ford excused his own brand of capitalism by pointing out that "the manufacturer, the manager of work, the provider of tools and justice is not the capitalist in the real sense. . . . He himself must go to capitalists for the money with which to finance his plans."

The first ten anti-Semitic articles were mild compared to what was to follow, but the advent of the series took everyone by surprise. The magazine had been established more than a year before the attacks began, and at the inception of the publication most accepted it at face value as Henry Ford's personal platform for expressing his crusade for right living. "I have definite ideas and ideals that I believe are practical for the good of all, and intend giving them to the public without having them garbled, distorted or misquoted," Ford had said when he bought the small country weekly newspaper, *The Dearborn Independent*.[7] He named himself president, his wife Clara vice-president, and his son Edsel secretary-treasurer, keeping the operation out of the accounting of the Ford Motor Company.

During that first year the magazine was numbingly dull. It extolled all the rural virtues of thrift, hard work, and moral integrity and offered little else. It did take a strong stand supporting Woodrow Wilson's League of Nations and was clearly in favor of women's rights, but these subjects were not controversial enough to carry a weekly publication. And on all other issues,

15

the publication's provinciality came through loud and clear. It criticized New York actresses for daring to expose undergarments in bedroom scenes. It attacked "orgies and bacchanalian revels, Babylons of jazz, and the evils of drink." Wall Street was the arch villain in its early melodramatic prose, such as the article "What I Found in Wall Street, by a Girl Who Spent Five Years in a Broker's Office." Her own innocence, her hopes and ideals had been deflowered by the financiers. The editorial page, which was simply dubbed "Mr. Ford's Own Page," spoke mostly of opportunity for hardworking young people. "Opportunity will not overlook you because you wear overalls" was a common theme.

Henry Ford took a personal hand in *The Dearborn Independent* and marked it quickly as an extension of his personality. The paper actually was being produced from an engineering laboratory alongside his tractor plant. The writers, all of whom had to punch time clocks, he called "good mechanics" when they expressed Ford's views. True to his spirit, he wanted to approach everything from a mass production concept. He suggested that stories be written in assemblyline fashion, with one person writing the story outline, another adding on the humor, and still another the editorial comment. Somehow the writers managed to talk him out of that idea.[8] Most newspapers and magazines ignored the existence of *The Dearborn Independent*. Those that commented on it were less than kind. *The American* wrote of the "trite truths of Henry Ford's new weekly paper."[9] *Saturday Night* called it the "best weekly ever turned out by a tractor plant,"[10] and *The Detroit Times* said the publication "doesn't fit the genius of Ford."[11] The publication was such a disappointment during that first year that an outside consultant, J. J. O'Neil, was called in to advise how to spice it up. The publica-

16

tion, O'Neil said in his fourteen-page report, lacks coherence and force. If it is to be the "chronicle of neglected truth," then it must become fearless and independent. "One single series may make us known to millions," O'Neil said, emphasizing, "Let's have some sensationalism."[12] While some have suggested that O'Neil's report may have stirred Ford into initiating the Jew-baiting series, it is clear that Ford made up his mind even before the establishment of his magazine to attack them. His personal secretary and general manager of *The Dearborn Independent* said that staff members were hired and told first that "Ford's going to start in on the Jews."[13] It appears that Ford was not the least concerned about the financial losses of the publication and was simply waiting for it to become established before launching his program.

The crew Henry Ford put together to carry out his campaign was impressive. He virtually drained the largest newspaper in Detroit, the *Detroit News*, hiring away eight top men. The first to be hired was Edwin G. Pipp, who had been with the *News* for sixteen years, serving as foreign correspondent, managing editor, and editor-in-chief. Pipp was an outspoken liberal who had believed completely in Henry Ford's idealism in the early months. Pipp brought in seven other *Detroit News* staffers, but when the anti-Semitic articles began, he quit Ford in disgust, establishing his own paper, *Pipp's Weekly*, to counter Ford's efforts. Pipp, a Catholic, could not tolerate religious bigotry, nor could most of the people he had brought with him to Ford. After the first year of Jew-baiting articles, only two of the original eight remained.

One of the writers Pipp had brought from the *Detroit News* stayed and took charge of the *Dearborn Independent* upon Pipp's sudden departure. He was William J. Cameron, the man who was to become Henry Ford's voice for the next two decades. He was a columnist at the *Detroit News,* a man his colleagues nicknamed "the walking dictionary." Largely self-educated, Cameron was exceedingly well read and had an impressive mastery of rhetoric. One observer put it, "Cameron was the intellectual center of the Ford empire, outranking his colleagues by the force of his spirit."[14] He was also a deeply religious man, having been a preacher for six years in a rural Michigan village. Even after he joined the Ford staff, Cameron made once-a-week visits to a poor people's mission in Detroit where he delivered warm and moving sermonettes.[15] Cameron was an evangelist who, having spent most of his life wrestling with his own alcoholism, seemed to have a remarkable compassion for the problems of others. All of those who knew him then were impressed by his easygoing, amiable nature. Even Philip Slomovitz, who worked with Cameron at the *News* and later opposed him and the *Independent* from his own chair as editor of the *Detroit Jewish News,* called him a charming man. "He often appeared at Jewish meetings back then," Slomovitz said, "and he was always supportive of our community."[16]

Ford, accustomed to firing on the spot any employee with a trace of alcohol on his breath, tolerated Cameron's drinking problem because he could do something few others could—interpret Henry Ford's meandering statements. Ford's mind did not follow logical tracks, but leaped about so haphazardly that even his closest associates found it impossible at times to understand the gist of his reasoning. Fred Black, a *Dearborn Independent* staffer, remembered, "Journalists would come away from interviews scratching their heads, then go to Cameron and ask, 'What in the hell did the old man mean by this?' "[17] Cameron acted as Ford's interpreter, which made him

18

the key man on the *Dearborn Independent* and the only man who could express Ford's thoughts on "Mr. Ford's Own Page."

Cameron also wrote most of the anti-Semitic articles. He resisted at first. Pipp recalled how Cameron told him on the way to work that "Ford has been at me to commence writing on those cursed Jewish articles. I don't know what to write." According to Pipp, Cameron talked back to Ford, something unheard-of within the company, throwing out "biting bits of sarcasm and giving vent to expressions of utmost disgust" at the prospect of the Jewish articles.[18] At one point, Cameron was sent to the Detroit Public Library to gather information on the Jews to use against them in the articles. He came back even more upset. Pipp said he reported "what a wonderful race they were, and how little he had known of their history, and what a magnificent history it was."[19] Yet as Cameron wrote article after article condemning the Jews, he became infected with his own poison. Soon it was clear that Cameron believed what he was writing, and, as we shall see later, he became a leading anti-Semite throughout the twenties and thirties. How this radical transformation came about is perhaps one of the most curious aspects of the early campaign.

Ernest Liebold, Ford's personal secretary, needed no such convincing. He was willingly anti-Semitic. Liebold's aggressive anti-Semitism appears in numerous letters throughout the Ford archives, letters in which he was speaking on Ford's behalf. Pipp related one instance in which a member of the *Dearborn Independent* staff asked about the rumor that there had been a change in the relationship in Mexico between the government and priests. "Oh, I understand all that," Liebold had said. "The Jew moneylenders in Europe induced the pope to order his priests in Mexico to do so and so." Pipp, in fact, laid Ford's anti-Semitism to Liebold, saying that while he doubted if Ford could determine the point at which he became anti-Semitic, he was certain Liebold could. Fred Black, a short-term *Dearborn Independent* employee and longtime Ford man, later said in his *Reminiscences* that Liebold could say the nastiest things about the Jews. "You could tell it was part of his whole makeup—he was anti-Semitic." On the Jewish articles, he once bragged that "when we get through with the Jews, there won't be one of them who will dare raise his head in public."[20] Liebold himself, while denying his anti-Semitism, expressed it repeatedly in his own reminiscences. He told one story about a Jewish *Dearborn Independent* employee, Ida Steinberg, and how she was given a swastika pin, one of 100 sent to Liebold from Germany. Ida wore it home and was rebuked by her family. Liebold comforted her and said he told her, "Let it roll like water off a duck's back."[21] The anecdote is significant, for it appears his anti-Semitism may have had a great deal to do with his pro-German ideology. Liebold's father came from Germany, and it was apparent that he was proud of his ancestry. When Prince Louis Ferdinand, the Kaiser's grandson, visited Ford, he said Liebold greeted him in broken German and raved about being German.[22] Liebold spoke enthusiastically about German accomplishments and downplayed any Jewish contributions. He made it a point to call Einstein a German and to ignore the physicist's Jewish heritage.[23]

Liebold's anti-Semitism is important, because in the unstructured world of the Ford empire, he was second in power to Ford himself. There was no formally acknowledged hierarchial order in the Ford Motor Company. Titles meant nothing; Ford himself never had one. From the moment he was hired by Ford in 1911, Liebold gained power rapidly in the unstructured environment. He had Ford's ear and, in most cases, acted for Ford without ever consulting with him. Ford detested details and day-to-day business. If Liebold had not assumed responsibility, the operation of Ford's offices would have fallen into absolute chaos. Liebold became more of the company's general manager than a personal secretary. He bought up most of the mining property in the upper peninsula of Michigan and the Detroit, Toledo & Ironton (D.T.&I.) Railroad in Ford's name. He ran the *Dearborn Independent* and the Ford Hospital, where he made it a hard-and-fast rule that no Jewish physicians were allowed on staff.[24] And he was in charge of Ford's personal cash-on-hand in the vault across from his office, a sum that often amounted to well over $1 million in discretionary funds. Norman Hapgood, a leading journalist, noted at the time, "Liebold has such a stranglehold on his employer that he practically decides whom Mr. Ford shall see in all . . . matters . . . and he is likely to remain in the room during any conference in which he wishes himself to determine the outcome."[25] Even Ford's wife and his son Edsel, president and part owner of the company, could not override Liebold's influence. Most historians agree that both Mrs. Ford and Edsel were strongly opposed to the anti-Semitic articles, yet Liebold was in favor of them, and they persisted. Liebold, it seems, was Ford's favorite because he would carry out orders with which most men would refuse to soil their hands.[26] He was Ford's hatchet man, firing anyone who offended the boss in the slightest manner. Fred Black recalled how Liebold had advised him how to get ahead within the company: "You be in a position where you don't give a goddamn what happens to anybody." Harry Bennett, who later became Ford's chief henchman, said, "Liebold looked like a Prussian. [Henry Ford] had a gestapo of his own within Ford Motor Company." Liebold, Bennett main-

21

tained, kept elaborate files and had some information on everyone in the organization.[27]

"Gestapo" may have been a remarkably apt term, at least in describing Liebold's secret army of detectives. Liebold established a network of prominent investigators, many of whom were former U.S. Secret Service and Army Intelligence agents, to spy on the acitivities of American Jews, attempting to get anything on them which could be linked to the international-conspiracy theory or simply used to smear them in the *Dearborn Independent*. The names of these primary secret agents were well known and respected in their day. C. C. Daniels, a New York lawyer and brother of the secretary of the navy, was Liebold's secret agent in New York, drawing $1,000 a month plus expenses in retainers. Dr. Harris Houghton, a Ford functionary, was the former head of the U.S. Army intelligence-gathering bureau in New York. F. Hunter Creech, a respected lawyer in Washington, D.C., and former Secret Service agent, was also on the Ford secret payroll. Charles Smith and Paul E. Tuthill, both former Secret Service agents, were Ford agents as well. Stanley F. Finch, associate to the U.S. Attorney General at the time, was also on the team. Liebold also employed a German detective, Lars Jacobsen, as a secret agent. On one mission to contact the ex-kaiser for information, Jacobsen wrote to Liebold, warning him to use utmost caution in any communication: "I have no delusions about what the Jewish revolutionary party in Germany will do to me if they find out that I am communicating with the Hohenzollerns on behalf of Mr. Ford, in order to secure information that will show the Jews up."[28]

Liebold made a cloak-and-dagger game out of directing Ford's secret detective forces. Everyone had a code number. Daniels was 120X, Creech 123X, Smith 124X, and Liebold himself was agent

121X. Each primary agent hired as many additional detectives as needed, reporting these outlays simply as office expenses. When a secondary agent was used, he, too, was given a code designation, such as 102AB, 103AB, and so on. Liebold also developed a phrase code to further mask his communications. "OBLU" meant "Acknowledge receipt of check," and "OCMI" meant "Wire results." The best message was "ACADAM," which meant "Mr. Ford says O.K."[29]

The detective activities touched most of the prominent Jews of the day. Detectives infiltrated parties where Otto Kahn, the banking magnate, or Jacob Schiff, noted Jewish philanthropist, might be present. They investigated any important organization which had any member who looked as if he might be a Jew, or even if the organization might be involved with Jews. The Civil Liberties Bureau, the American Relief Association, the U.S. Shipping Board, and the War Finance Corporation all came under scrutiny, largely because someone employed there had a Jewish-sounding name or a prominent nose. Gentiles with liberal leanings were also investigated as probable "Jewish fronts." Three U.S. presidents, Herbert Hoover, Howard Taft, and Woodrow Wilson, were suspected of being Jewish fronts and were thoroughly investigated by Ford's men. If the work of these detectives was not so insidious, it might have been amusing at times. Creech and his operatives, for example, spent weeks trying to figure out whether Supreme Court Justice Louis Brandeis, a Jew, had a private telephone hooked up directly to the White House. A simple visit to the justice's office was too direct, so all manner of intrigue was invented to determine if such a line existed—which, of course, it did not.[30]

As the early anti-Semitic articles ran in the *Dearborn Independent* and Liebold's secret agents snooped, Jew haters of all kinds came out of the shadows with offers and information. One of these men was New York lawyer Maurice Leon, a Jew of French ancestry, who believed that German Jews had been at the head of an international conspiracy during the world war. Leon followed leading Jews and developed a cross-index file on each. If, for instance, Jacob Schiff went to a party, everyone who attended the party was thereafter followed, and a new cross-index developed on that suspect. Leon's information found its way to Liebold's staff, and was much appreciated. As Hapgood says, "There is good reason to believe that the *Dearborn Independent* vision of the Jewish world conspiracy, headed by a few dictators at the top, had its origin in this elaborate cross-index of Mr. Leon."[31]

Another typical supportive response came from an organization called The Patriotic American Patriot [sic] in Brooklyn, N.Y., which offered Ford the following suggestion for legislation:

> Be it enacted by the Congress of our United States; That on and after the passage of this BILL, it will be UNLAWFUL, for any person or persons, male or female, white or colored, native or foreign born; to hold any National, State or Municipal Government Office, either ELECTIVE or APPOINTIVE, for pay or otherwise; or having any Voting Franchise whatsoever; or own any Real Estate, or transact any Business whatsoever; or own any Bonds, Stocks, Securities, Mortgages, etc.; or to hold any Meeting or Meetings, or Service or Services whatsoever, not consistent with the Grace of God; or any Teaching or Teachings other than the Teachings of Jesus Christ; or enter our United States from any other Country whatsoever; WHO ARE NOT FIRM BELIEVERS IN ALMIGHTY GOD OUR HEAVENLY FATHER, AND HIS SON, OUR LORD AND SAVIOUR, JESUS CHRIST, and THE CONSTITUTION OF OUR UNITED STATES.

The PENALTY for Violation of this Law, will be, from one to five years in Prison and Confiscation of ALL the Real Estate and other Property and Business, in which he, she or they, have any interest whatsoever. Any Law inconsistent herewith is hereby declared Rescinded, and Null and Void.

By the passage of this Bill, it AUTOMATICALLY APPLIES RETRO-ACTIVELY to each and every person in our United States at the time of its passage.

PRAY CONGRESS: SAVE OUR UNITED STATES FROM ANTI-CHRIST INVASION.

Perhaps the most important individual to come out of the shadows and join the Ford anti-Semitic crew was Boris Brasol. He was a young, remarkably handsome Russian tsarist who had been a leading member of the anti-Semitic Black Hundred society in his native country. He called himself the second greatest preliminary investigator in Russia and boasted that he had studied criminology in Germany, France, Switzerland, and England. Brasol was a remarkably flexible secret agent at one time or another for just about everyone. He went from employment in the tsarist government to an agent of the U.S. Army Military Intelligence division in 1918. Later, in the 1930s and early 1940s, he was to become an agent of the Nazi regime. But in 1920 he came to Dearborn and so impressed Liebold with his anti-Semitic knowledge that he was immediately put on the payroll as a writer. William Cameron, not yet indoctrinated into the Jew hatred, said in a letter to a New York detective that Brasol was indeed on the Ford payroll, but that his information about the Jews was incorrect, adding, "Are all Russian officers such liars as Brasol?"[32] Before long, Cameron would be using Brasol's lies as the basis for most of his articles.

One story of Brasol's Russian background will suffice to illustrate his character. The son of a Christian prostitute in Kiev was killed by several of the woman's street associates. The chief of detectives, Minschuk, had the evidence and was preparing the case when Brasol and fellow members of the Black Hundred concocted the tale that the boy had been killed by Jews and his blood drained for a religious ritual. The police chief protested and was sent off to jail for a year. A Jewish bookkeeper named Mendal Beylis was arrested for the crime, and awaited trial for eighteen months while the Black Hundred attempted to build a case. The strange trial consisted mainly of proving that there was such a thing as ritual murder. The jury, consisting of both peasants and professional people, brought in the curious verdict that yes, Jewish ritual murders did exist, but no, Beylis had not participated in one. Newspapers across Russia protested the ridiculous conclusion, and Brasol's associates went to work closing down fourteen newspapers and fining twenty-two others for objecting to the proceedings at Kiev. Later in America, Brasol would recount the tale of the trial, bemoaning the fact that the prosecution failed to convict the Jew, even while admitting openly that the man was innocent.

In the *Dearborn Independent*'s employ, Brasol could far more effectively spread his anti-Semitic propaganda. He wrote for the publication for nearly two years and remained in close contact with Ford's top people until World War II. Brasol also brought in some of his tsarist friends to join the Ford team, one of them Major-General Count Cherep Spiridovich, who became a subscription agent for the paper. In 1921 Brasol wrote to Spiridovich, boasting, "Within the last year I have written three books, two of which have done the Jews more injury than would have been done to them by ten pogroms."[33] It is worth noting here that during Brasol's tenure on Liebold's team, actual pogroms were discussed seriously among the Ford secret agent crew. Brasol was later quoted as saying: "There are going to be the biggest pogroms and massacres here and elsewhere; I will write and I will precipitate them."[34]

Brasol's greatest contribution to the *Dearborn Independent* was his introduction of the *Protocols of the Learned Elders of Zion.* He sold them to Liebold as if they were esoteric and mystical documents, even though the *Protocols* were openly being sold at the time in Russia and France. The *Protocols,* purportedly written by Jews at the Zionist Congress at Basel, Switzerland, in 1897, outlined a worldwide plot to destroy the Aryan nations by providing leadership and financial backing to every activity which would undermine the social and moral institutions of the gentile world. There was, according to the *Protocols,* a single Jewish Sanhedrin, or supreme council, directing the actions of Jews everywhere. The *Protocols* contained twenty-four sets of instructions, ostensibly given in a lecture to the younger Jewish conspirators. The document was an absurd forgery, developed by Serge Nilus, a tsarist agent, for the purpose of inspiring pogroms in Russia. And Nilus had not even been original, plagiarizing the Protocols from a mid-nineteenth-century novel by a French lawyer, Maurice Joly, *Dialogue in Hell Between Machiavelli and Montesquieu,* a satirical attack on French political powers. Over the next twenty years, the *Protocols* would be exposed again and again as rank forgeries, beginning in 1921 by the *London Times.*[35] In a major court case in Switzerland in 1935 they were finally discussed openly. Germany's Lieutenant-Colonel Fleischhauer argued that they were authentic beyond question. The president of the court concluded: "I am convinced that the *Protocols* are obscene literature and, more than that, namely, ridiculous nonsense."[36]

Despite repeated verdicts of a hoax, the *Protocols* had a rich, full life, and even appear in anti-Semitic literature today. Hugo Valentin, an expert on anti-Semitic literature, has concluded of the *Protocols*: "It is no exaggeration to say that they cost the lives of many thousands of innocent persons and that more blood and tears cling to their pages than to those of any other mendacious document in the world's history."[37]

Brasol brought the *Protocols* first to Dr. Harris Houghton, who was then with U.S. Army Intelligence. Houghton, later to become a Ford anti-Semitic agent himself, had them translated by a member of his office, Natalie DeBogory, daughter of a well-known Russian general, who would later work with C. C. Daniels, a Ford spy. Once translated, they were taken to Liebold, who was offered not only a copy of the *Protocols*, but, for a price, the "originals." In his reminiscences, Liebold says he turned down the originals because "We'd have to prove their authenticity."[38]

Here, at last, was the document Henry Ford had awaited. It proved beyond a doubt his suspicion that the Jews were behind it all. Every evil, every disruption, every distortion of the old agrarian moral code could now be attributed to a single archenemy— the Jews did it. The *Dearborn Independent* quickly picked up on the *Protocols* and, for the remainder of the series of articles, used them as the source of absolute authority.

The *Dearborn Independent* did not print the *Protocols* in toto in any single issue. If they had, the absurdity of the document would have mocked their effort. Instead, Cameron and his assistants put them into a contemporary setting. A modern situation, such as the Bolshevik Revolution, was detailed, then laid to the Jews with one of the *Protocols* as the final abiding evidence. This format lent a far stronger appearance of legitimacy, which is why Ford's *International Jew* had much wider acceptance than the *Protocols* themselves.

In the tenth article of the ninety-one in the *Dearborn Independent* series, the *Protocols* were introduced for the first time. They appeared together with emphasis that the *Protocols* depended on the corruptibility of gentile nature and that the Jews would triumph, not through actions, but by *words*, literally talking a path to hell. Article after article could now proceed to show the subversion conspiracy. The Jews had started the world war in order to profit by it. Bolshevism was a Jewish invention, as were liberalism and unionism. When Arthur Brisbane, Hearst editor, came to the Jews' defense, arguing that there could not be a world program since the Jews are leaders in diametrically opposing areas from democracy to communism, the *Dearborn Independent* now had the answer. The Ninth *Protocol* said:

> People of all opinions and all doctrines are at our service, restorers of monarchy, demagogues, Socialists, Communists, and other Utopians. We have put them all to work. Every one of them from his point of view is undermining the last remnant of authority, is trying to overthrow all existing order. All the governments have been tormented by these actions. But we will not give them peace until they recognize our supergovernment.

Jews were behind everything that Henry Ford and the Populist farmer were against, the paper trumpeted. Jews created amusement parks like Coney Island, which, the *Independent* maintained, were "the centers of nervous thrills and looseness." Negro jazz somehow became "Yiddish moron music" in the publication's vernacular. "Sports clothes and flashy jewelry," as

29

well as every possible luxury, were Jewish corrupting devices. The movies were a Jewish monopoly and had been downgraded by the low moral standards of these "Asiatic" people. "The reels were reeking of filth. They are slimy with sex plays. They are overlapping one another with crime." The Jews controlled the press (a personal vendetta of Ford's) for the purpose of "keeping certain things out of the public mind and putting certain things into it."

No American institution, it seemed, was above their corrupting influence. The Jews took over baseball, making it a fixed betting activity instead of the all-American sport. The Jews gained control of the liquor business, replacing the high-quality bourbon whiskey with cheap and vile "blended" stock. All crime was related to something that resembled a Jewish Mafia. Bootlegging was a special province because rabbis had been exempted from Prohibition in order to use and distribute ceremonial wine. Jews even took advantage of Jews in the disgusting existence of New York tenaments. They had infiltrated the Freemasons, using the organization as a Jewish tool. And every time a Jew suggested using nonsectarian language in schools or public places, the *Dearborn Independent* used the incident as proof that the Jews were attempting to eliminate Christianity from "this Christian country." One close observer of Ford's propaganda wrote, "It appealed to every passion, charged the Jews as a 'race' with every crime calculated to rouse the frenzied anger of the non-Jewish population."[39]

The *Dearborn Independent* even assumed the responsibility of rewriting American history to conform to Ford's distorted perception of it. Christopher Columbus, we are told, was not the first European to set foot on this continent; it was a Jewish interpreter, Luis de Torres, who first came ashore. The *Inde-*

pendent tells us de Torres was the first to find and exploit tobacco—a heinous evil, according to Ford. Queen Isabella was a Jewish front, the money for the New World expedition actually coming from three secret Jews who profited by the venture. Haym Solomon, who supported the American Revolution with his entire fortune, was transformed by the *Independent* into a war instigator and profiteer. And Benedict Arnold, the man Henry Ford thought was a writer when interviewed on the witness stand, turns out to be an unfortunate pawn of Jewish moneylenders who would not have betrayed his country if it were not for their sinister influence.

Above all else, the Jews seemed guilty because they refused to give up their Jewishness and become complete Americans. "There is all the difference in the world between an American Jew and a Jewish American," the *Independent* wrote. They did not acclimate themselves to American traditions, but looked to a foreign government, the Zionist government which respected no boundries or traditions. Yet they would go to all sorts of devious means, such as "the gentle art of changing Jewish names," to appear like gentiles. And then, when they gained power, their entire purpose was to eradicate Christian virtues.[40] All liberalism and variation from rural American folkways, then, were suspect. The underlying message was clear: Beware of progress; it's a Jewish scheme.

Henry Ford believed all of the "facts" his detectives brought to him and, as Pipp later said, "refused to listen to any logic." Anyone in the organization who openly disagreed with his anti-Semitic campaign was eventually purged. That included top men such as Frank Klingensmith, a vice-president and company treasurer who had helped James Couzens set up Ford Motor Company. 'Klingensmith used to line up with a lot of

31

Jewish bankers," Liebold explained. "And, besides, the ex-treasurer was half Jewish."[41] Warren C. Anderson, head of Ford in Europe, was brought back to the United States because he had made "repeated entreaties, appeals, and finally demands that the Jewish attacks cease." Liebold dismissed him. Eventually even Alfred Lucking, Ford's legal right hand who had guided him through the Dodge case, the *Chicago Tribune* trial, and the Senator Newberry battle, was purged because he spoke out against Ford's anti-Semitism.[42] Ford became obsessed with the Jews, talking about them almost constantly. One longtime Ford employee, Harold Hicks, tells the story of the time the company received a new brass-fitted dynamometer, which Hicks was installing. A supervisor, Roy Schumann, said, "Don't ever let Mr. Ford see you use any brass, because brass is a Jew metal. You'll have to paint that black."[43]

To the press, Ford became more openly hostile. After all, they were part of the Jewish plot. He expressed himself on the Jews at every opportunity. When some of his tractors were seized in Berlin because of import restrictions, he told a New York news-paperman, "I'll blame it on the Jewish businessmen—you blame it on anyone you want."[44] He consented to two biographies during this period. One was a puffed-up book by James Martin Miller that defended Ford's stand against the Jews; the work incorporated many allegations from the *Dearborn Independent* and sought to buttress them. Ford was depicted as a crusader for truth against a Jewish conspiracy afraid to see the undisputable facts aired in public. Miller's book was a best seller. But its sales paled beside those of Henry Ford's autobiography, *My Life and Work,* which made its debut in 1922. Here Ford repeated his charges, only in a much more subdued tone. He wrote:

32

An impartial investigation of the last war, of what preceded it and what has come out of it, would show beyond a doubt that there is in the world a group of men with vast powers of control, that prefers to remain unknown, that does not seek office or any of the tokens of power, that belongs to no nation whatever but is international—a force that uses every government, every wide-spread business organization, every agency of publicity, every resource of national psychology, to throw the world into panic for the sake of getting still more power over the world.

And Ford's antagonism against the Jews as being nonproducers comes through just as clearly:

There is in this country a sinister element that desires to creep in between the men who work with their hands and the men who think and plan for the men who work with their hands. The same influence that drove the brains, experience, and ability out of Russia is busily engaged in raising prejudice here.[45]

Through all of this, Ford tenaciously denied any prejudice against the Jews or wish to harm them. In a strange sense, he was correct. Ford defended his articles as "a course of instruction on the Jews," which he said would have to last five years to be effective. He had only to subject the good Jews to the light of truth, and they would purge their ranks of the bad Jews he wrote about. "These articles have always held that the cleansing must come from within Judah itself," the *Dearborn Independent* held. As Miller, his apologist, wrote, "His purpose was to let the air and sunlight of open and frank discussion into a question that was existing in whispers and suspicion. He saw from the beginning that the Jews themselves would be the greatest beneficiaries

33

of this work. He felt that if even one man was fearless enough, and frank enough, and fair enough, and well-informed enough to show a certain type of Jew what figure he cut in American opinion, it would open up the way for those Jews' self-correction."[46]

Ford could never understand why Jews might be offended by his attacks. One of his old friends and a former neighbor, Rabbi Leo Franklin, had received a new Model T from Henry every year. When the anti-Semitic articles appeared, Rabbi Franklin sent the car back the day it was delivered. Ford was surprised and called the rabbi to ask, "What's wrong, Dr. Franklin? Has anything come between us?"[47] Ford continued to employ 3,000 or more Jews in his plants, but he kept them in physical labor positions, saw that they worked, and didn't let them get into office jobs.[48] Philip Slomovitz, who had numerous occasions to go through Ford plants during those years as the editor of Detroit's *Jewish News*, was always struck by the number of Jews who would come up to him and say, "Henry Ford is a great man. He has always treated us well." The truth seems to be that Ford, who genuinely liked people, was sometimes able to separate his antagonism for Jewry from the individuals involved. It was the same Henry Ford who told Liebold, "You can't single them out. You have to go after them all. They are all part of the same system."[49] Who, when he befriended a Jew on the job, would explain it to Bennett, "Oh, he's mixed. He's not all Jewish."[50]

Reactions to Ford's anti-Semitic campaign, the first of its kind in American history, came from all quarters. Mass meetings were conducted across the country in protest. In Toledo on April 1, 1921, sales of the *Dearborn Independent* precipitated a gang fight on the street in front of the Federal Building. Traffic was blocked for over an hour and four men were arrested.[51] In

Cincinnati, the City Council responded to the public outcry by passing a law which banned inflammatory publications, effectively blocking *Dearborn Independent* sales. Police in Boston stopped sales of the *Dearborn Independent* during the summer of 1921 but, unsure of their legal rights, soon backed off. A minor riot in Pittsburgh led the police to ban sales of inflammatory material. In New York City there was so much harassment of *Dearborn Independent* sales that Ford's lawyers had to obtain an injunction in order to distribute. Many public libraries banned the publication, and when they didn't, copies were stolen and destroyed.[52] Liebold complained about this, blaming it naturally on Jews (for once, he was probably right).[53] The American Civil Liberties Union wrote to the mayors of major cities asking that the *Dearborn Independent* be barred from public sales.[54] A protest resolution was entered in Congress. Some prominent Jews made light of the attacks. Bernard Baruch had been named by the *Dearborn Independent* as the most powerful of the cabal, the "Jew of superpower" and the "proconsul of Judah in America" during the world war. When asked about the charges by reporters, he simply smiled and said, "Now, boys, you wouldn't expect me to deny them, would you?"[55]

Major organizations and individuals answered indirectly by reaffirming their tolerance and respect for American Jews. The Federal Council of the Church of Christ in America met in Boston in December of 1920 and passed the following resolution:

> Whereas, for some time past there have been in circulation in this country publications tending to create race prejudice and arouse animosity against our Jewish fellow-citizens and containing charges so preposterous as to be unworthy of credence, be it resolved that the Federal Council of the Churches of Christ in

35

America, impressed by the need at this period of our national existence for unity and brotherhood, deplores all such cruel and unwarranted attacks upon our Jewish brethren and in a spirit of good-will extends to them an expression of confidence in their patriotism and their good citizenship and earnestly admonishes our people to express disapproval of all actions which are conducive to intolerance.[56]

An even more impressive group was formed to counter Ford's anti-Semitism. John Spargo, educator and prominent author, enlisted more than 100 fellow non-Jews to express their concern. Among the names of the signers were President Woodrow Wilson and former President William Howard Taft. While the letter did not speak to Ford directly, its aim was clear:

The loyalty and patriotism of our fellow citizens of the Jewish faith is equal to that of any part of our people, and requires no defense at our hands. . . . Anti-Semitism is almost invariably found closely intertwined with other sinister forces, particularly those which are corrupt, reactionary and oppressive. We believe that it should not be left to men and women of Jewish faith to fight this evil, but that it is in a very special sense the duty of citizens who are not Jews by ancestry or faith.[57]

Dr. Leo Franklin, Ford's old friend, worked especially hard to dissuade him from his attacks. Franklin was a strong advocate of Christian-Jewish fellowship, and had been awarded an honorary doctorate from the University of Detroit, the largest Catholic university in Michigan. The rabbi was deeply hurt by Ford's actions and attempted repeatedly to communicate with him, through both personal letters and open letters in Detroit's newspapers. He tried in vain to reverse Ford's beliefs. "If there is to be a change in the financial system of the world," Franklin argued, "I do not think that Jews more than others should be consulted. Some Jews have, it is true, shown a genius for finance, but it is not a universal trait, and many of the great financiers have been non-Jews. . . . If he [Ford] wishes to gain the confidence of the world, Jew and non-Jew, he should frankly state that he knows now what he printed was false: that the so-called *Protocols of the Elders of Zion* upon which his attacks are based, were . . . forgeries. All men, Jew or Gentile, would be glad to know that Ford has had the courage to admit he has been wrong."[58]

To his pleas, Franklin received only a curt reply from Ernest Liebold regretting that Franklin had felt it necessary to sever Ford's friendship, but adding, "I sincerely hope, however, that conditions will so adjust themselves as to eventually convince yourself that Mr. Ford's position is correct, as resulting therefrom the world and all its people may benefit thereby."[59]

Louis Marshall of the American Jewish Committee, and a leading civil rights leader of his day, also attempted to answer Ford's charges, at first. Marshall, a partner in the New York law firm of Guggenheimer, Untermeyer, and Marshall, had built a reputation for defending the rights not only of his fellow Jews but also of blacks, Japanese, and Hindus. He was a highly assimilated Reform Jew, who personally had publicly rejected the idea of the Zionist homeland. Marshall wrote numerous rebuttal letters calling to Ford's attention that the Jews "numerically constitute less than one percent of the population of the earth; and more than one-half of them are on the verge of starvation." He answered Ford's charges that the Russian revolution was an all-Jewish plot, pointing out that "the originators of Bolshevism were exclusively non-Jews. While it is true that there are Jews among the Bolshevists, notably Trotsky, they represent a small fraction of the Jews of the followers of Bolshevism. Lenin, who belonged to the Russian aristocracy and has not a drop of Jewish blood in his veins, was the creator as he has been the motive power of the Soviets." And on the Ford charges that the Masonic Order had been infiltrated and was dominated by Jews for more than a hundred years, Marshall simply remarked that fifteen presidents of the U.S. had been Freemasons, including George Washington.[60] Yet all of these replies were ignored in Dearborn, prompting Marshall to encourage the American Jewish Committee to simply act as if the *Dearborn Independent* didn't exist, since any further counterthrust "would only serve to give publicity to these articles which they otherwise would not have."[61]

The Ford dealers could not ignore the *Dearborn Independent*'s campaign, first because it led to an unofficial boycott of the purchase of Ford vehicles and secondly because they were pressured into selling the publication for Henry Ford. Jewish individuals and firms immediately stopped buying Fords. Many gentile firms stopped buying Fords as well, some out of sympathy for the Jews and other to appease Jewish customers. When a 400-car parade was assembled in Hartford, Connecticut, to honor Albert Einstein and Chaim Weizmann, the order went out that there would be "positively no Ford machines permitted in line."[62] While the boycott had little effect in rural communities where Ford's sales were strongest, it was clear that it was devastating sales in the major metropolitan areas with significant Jewish populations. There was a dramatic drop in total Ford sales in late 1920, and while some of the decline could be laid to a decline in the economy that year, a measure had to be attributed to the Jewish boycott. Even the humorist Will Rogers quipped that the boycott "may not be a complete success yet—but it will be as soon as someone learns how to make a cheaper car."[63]

Dealers reacted. Many of them, like Gaston Plaintiff, a New York sales manager and personal friend of Ford, wrote letters complaining of the sales decline. Henry Ford's only answer was, "If they want our product, they'll buy it." Liebold was far more sarcastic in his responses to the dealers. When a Virginia dealer, E. C. Lindsay, wrote to say that his Jewish landlord was threatening eviction because of the articles, Liebold replied, "Does it not appear to you that a Ford agent should own his building to place him beyond the exertion of such pressure! We naturally expect, and our agents must also feel, that the Jews will endeavor to make victims of them whenever possible."[64] In an even more revealing letter to Mr. Plaintiff, Liebold wrote that "the matter has gone too far for us to stop and consider now just where it is wrong. This has been a carefully weighed and considered long before we started. If anything we are publishing is untruthful, the Jews have thus far failed to show it. . . . I have found that the moment we open ourselves and extend interviews to the Jews, it is only used for the purpose of misquoting and publicity which has no bearing whatever on the issue and attempts to deride the individual members of our organization. So far as Mr. Ford is concerned, he has nothing to say to anybody. The matter is being handled entirely by the organization of the publishing company, and so long as Mr. Ford personally keeps out of it, I am confident that it can be brought to a successful end." In the same letter, Liebold answers the criticism that the *Protocols* are rank forgeries by stating, "If you will carefully read our articles, you will find we have at no time guaranteed their authenticity. We have merely stated that they contain and have paralleled this with what actually took place and are leaving it to the mind of the public to judge."[65] This, of course, is a long way from the *Dearborn Independent*'s frequent affirmation that "the statements offered in this series are never made without the strictest and fullest proof."

The dealers were forced not only to keep quiet and support Ford's stand, but to actively sell the *Dearborn Independent*. Sales had been dropping, and the publishing company tried many methods to bolster them—national advertising, enlisting schoolboys and church groups, and even hawking them from parked cars along the highway. None of this worked, so in a directive Ford then declared the *Dearborn Independent* to be as much a Ford product as the cars and trucks, and that dealers would distribute them. Ford placed ads in local newspapers to make it clear that the publication was, indeed, a Ford product. One statement in the ad read, "To begin with, the *Dearborn Independent* is Henry Ford's paper. There need be no uncertainty on that point. We understand that certain parties have given some dealers a different story, but be informed now that Mr. Ford's name at the top of the editorial page as president of the Dearborn Publishing Company means just what it says."[66]

With this "lead pipe" approach, circulation again climbed, pushing the half-million mark. A few dealers revoked their Ford franchises over the issue. The Barish Brothers of Sioux City, Iowa, dropped out dramatically by paying for a full-page advertisement in the local paper, explaining that there was no way they could support the *Dearborn Independent*'s stand and regretting that Ford considered the publication a Ford product.[67] Most dealers, however, with their life savings wrapped up in their businesses, acquiesced and sold both the cars and propaganda.

Not everyone attacked Ford's articles. Several newspapers

reprinted excerpts from the articles and praised Ford for printing them in the first place. The Ku Klux Klan was reviving at the time, and the anti-Semitic propaganda was welcome in those quarters. The *Dearborn Independent,* in fact, did a very positive piece on the K.K.K. and received a pleasant thank-you letter from the Imperial Emperor King Kleagle.[68] At about the same time the order of B'rith Abraham, meeting in Atlantic City at a convention, accused Henry Ford of also supplying financial support to the Klan, though this was never proven. The Klan's recitation of Ford's own words, however, is a matter of record. Imperial Wizard H. W. Evans, for example, quoted the *Dearborn Independent* before a Dallas audience in 1922. He said, "The Jew produces nothing anywhere on the face of the earth. He does not till the soil. He does not create or manufacture anything for common use. He adds nothing to the sum of human welfare."[69]

A startlingly large number of requests for copies of the *International Jew* came in to Ford then from people of all walks of life, and a remarkably large number of Christian ministers' requests for the anti-Semitic material are to be found throughout the Ford Archives' records.[70] Encouragement and supportive comments seemed to equal, if not outweigh, the negative reactions. Ford's appeal to bigotry brought him many friends.

But the skirmish was not to last. The first and most overt round of attacks ended in January 1922. Ford simply walked into the *Dearborn Independent* office and said stop. He wanted to fight the gold standard with a monetary reform program of his own, he said, and he believed he would need the Jews to help him succeed.

"They won't do it," Cameron said.

"Oh, yes they will; we can work them," Ford retorted.

"But we can do both," Liebold said.

"No we can't. Stop the Jewish articles," Ford said as he turned and walked out.[71]

It was not, of course, the end of his anti-Semitism—not by any means. He would continue to reprint copies of the *International Jew* in lots of 200,000 each. He even placed them on sale at the Ford Motor Company booth at the Michigan State Fair the following fall. And in a couple of years, the *Dearborn Independent* would be back at it again. But, for the moment, the barrage had stopped.

Was the monetary reform program the only reason? No one knows for sure. Allan Nevins, Ford's official biographer, suggests that Edsel Ford finally got up enough nerve to ask his father to stop the Jew-baiting and the old man complied. Considering how little influence Edsel had on his father, that theory is highly doubtful. Others point out the many eminent men who asked Ford to call a halt to his campaign. President Harding had first appealed to Ford through Louis Marshall and later through a friend, Judson Welliver, to stop. Nevins also suggests that Harding asked Thomas Edison and Arthur Brisbane, two men Ford greatly admired, to convince Ford to call off the attacks. And even Gaston Plaintiff, Ford's New York manager and friend, is credited by some with having talked Ford out of it because it was simply bad for business.

A rather delightful tale of why Ford desisted comes from Upton Sinclair's book *The Flivver King*. William Fox, a Hollywood motion-picture producer, heard that Ford was about to attack him in the *Dearborn Independent*. He sent a letter to Ford saying that he, too, was in the process of an investigation. Fox's newsreel service, which went to thousands of theaters twice a week, could be used to present footage of Ford cars involved in serious accidents. He had already instructed cameramen to start taking pictures of wrecks, especially ones where people were killed. The best pictures would appear on the screen. "The effect of this notice was immediate," Sinclair said. "Henry sent word back to William that he had decided to stop the attacks upon the Jews."[72]

This story, while intriguing, is suspect. Two major Jewish figures were already in the process of suing Ford for slander. Morris Gest filed a $5 million suit in California, and Lewis Berstein had a $1 million suit going against Ford in New York City. Gest, a theatrical producer, filed his suit because the *Independent* said he had neglected his poor parents after becoming famous. (The truth was his parents were rich.) And Berstein, a journalist, filed his suit because Ford had claimed he said Jews started the world war. Neither of these threats had deterred Ford, and it is unlikely that a menace such as the one Sinclair presents could have scared him either. Every counterthrust, including the Jewish boycott of his cars, seemed to result in even more bitter *Independent* attacks against the Jews.

The most plausible explanation for Ford's ceasefire comes from Edwin Pipp. Henry Ford was a candidate for president of the United States at the time. Ford-for-president clubs, more than 100 strong, had sprung up around the country. Straw votes showed Ford had a real chance to win, far greater than Harding. At first, Ford didn't seem to take the prospect seriously, but Liebold encouraged him. As Fred Black said, "Liebold was the main stimulation of the Ford-for-president boom. He expected to be the power behind the throne in Washington, as he was then in the company."[73] As a serious candidate, Pipp suggests, Ford began counting votes. In January, an advisor, whom Pipp doesn't name but who is probably Gaston Plaintiff, visited Ford and pinpointed the spots where the Jews refused to buy his cars—New York, Cincinnati, Cleveland, and other urban areas. If they wouldn't buy cars, they certainly wouldn't buy Ford for president. The advisor pointed out that under the electoral system no man had ever been elected who lost both Ohio and New York. Ford then supposedly recessed his anti-Semitic crusade for political reasons. While this argument makes sense, it assumes that Ford was completely set on becoming president. But the following year Ford had a meeting with Calvin Coolidge and ostensibly wrangled a deal whereby if Coolidge would back Ford's acquisition of the Muscle Shoals dam, the industrialist would throw his support to the president. Sinclair put it, " 'Keep cool with Coolidge' was the motto on which the Flivver King and the Klan proceeded to reelect their choice."[74] Given the tenacity with which Henry Ford went after any goal on which he set his sights, there is real doubt that he would have backed out of the race had he badly wanted the presidency.

All of these events could have influenced Ford, or none of them may have. Nor can we take Ford at his word that he wanted to enlist the help of the Jews to fight the gold standard, for although a couple of articles appeared in the *Independent* on the monetary reform issue after the Jew-baiting series, the new campaign lacked the fervor that was characteristic of a Ford-inspired push. In short, no one knows for sure why Henry Ford backed away. It is clear, however, that he was not through with the Jews. The *Dearborn Independent* crew continued to gather information on them for which use would be found later. The first volley was over, and Ford appeared to have lost little in power or popularity from the fray.

3

Hitler's Inspiration
•

Next to Adolph Hitler's desk at Nazi Party Headquarters in Munich hung a life-sized likeness of Henry Ford. On the table in the antechamber, visitors were often shocked to find anti-Semitic booklets and books with Henry Ford's name and portrait on the covers. They should not have been surprised, for in the National Socialist circles of both Munich and Berlin, Ford's name was invoked frequently and always with respect. A Hitler lieutenant named Christian Weber announced that if Ford ever came to Munich, he would be "received like a king."[1]

Hitler often spoke of Ford to his followers, frequently bragging about financial support he had received from the American industrialist.[2] With the press, Hitler was more guarded, yet at times he did express his adulation. When Ford was said to be running for president of the United States, for example, Hitler told *Chicago Tribune* reporter Raymond Fendrick that Ford had

100 percent of his support. "I wish," Hitler said, "that I could send some of my shock troops to Chicago and other big American cities to help in the elections. We look to Heinrich [Henry] Ford as the leader of the growing Fascist party in America."[3] His reverence for Ford did not wane, and in 1931 Hitler summarized his feelings when a *Detroit News* reporter asked what the portrait of Ford on Hitler's wall meant to him. "I regard Henry Ford as my inspiration," Hitler said.[4]

Hitler was not given to public adulation of those of non-German stock. His political posture simply would not permit it. Yet his admiration for Ford was both real and thoroughly understandable. Henry Ford's anti-Semitic propaganda which flowed into Germany lent credibility and reputability to Hitler's own.

In 1921, when tens of thousands of copies of the translation of Ford's *International Jew* were being distributed throughout Germany and Austria, Ford could be said to have had more influence with portions of those populations than Hitler's fledgling Nazi movement. Hitler had been a newcomer to the party, having joined in 1919, and did not take control of the movement until 1921. The National Socialist German Workers' Party was faltering, and few Germans took the movement, or the upstart former architectural student, seriously. Hitler would not make his first spectacular venture into politics until October 1923, and he later admitted that his *weltanschauung*—his outlook on the world—had not yet crystalized by then.

Henry Ford, on the other hand, was a folk hero in Germany as well as in America. The stories of Ford's five-dollar day and beneficent paternal attitude toward labor had been greeted warmly by German workers suffering in a depressed postwar economy. Part of his stature with German laborers derived from the stories of his stands against Wall Street financiers. In 1920,

Ford was in deep financial trouble. Instead of borrowing money, however, he forced his dealers to buy up a large car inventory, forcing *them* to borrow instead. The story was distorted in the retelling, showing Ford as the victim of greedy money men. It was a grand story for many susceptible Germans who pictured bankers as arch villains at the time. (Hitler told reporters later that this episode increased the support of the Nazis for their American hero.)

Numerous proofs of Ford's popularity in Germany are available. For example, when Ford announced plans to build a plant in the Reich, Germans stood in lines all night to buy his stock.[5] And when Ford's autobiography, *My Life and Work,* went on sale in Germany, it became that country's number-one best seller.[6] A new word entered the German lexicon: *Fordize* which meant to do things the Ford way, and to a desperate nation looking at this American's wealth and seeming compassion, to Fordize was the right way.

The admiration was mutual. Ford spoke highly of the German people. "I like Germans," he said. "They are talented and thrifty people. When I was a boy, I worked for a toolmaker from Germany. He taught me a lot of useful things."[7] From 1914 onward, Ford had been a close friend to Dr. Edward A. Rumely, a German-American accused in a U.S. Senate investigation of being the leader of German propaganda in America during the war. In 1918, Ford went to Washington, D.C., to use his influence in clearing Rumely of the charges.[8] (Rumely was to resurface in the late thirties as a suspected agent of the Third Reich.) One of Ernest Liebold's last duties for Ford was to develop a list of the great inventions and achievements of the German people. What Ford intended to do with this list is nowhere explained.[9] Ford was proud of befriending and hiring Germans, and when asked about his own nationality, would first say, "I am Dutch on my mother's side," even though he was predominantly of Irish-English ancestry.

The close ties between the fledgling German Nazi movement and Ford's *Dearborn Independent* were also apparent. The *Independent* frequently plagiarized the works of Werner Sombart, a Nazi economist.[10] In turn, it was believed that Ford's assistant, Ernest Liebold, shared his propaganda about the Jews with his friend Franz von Papen, later Vice-Chancelor of Germany in 1933 and 1934.[11] Casimir Palmer, a private investigator and former British military intelligence officer and one-time U.S. intelligence agent, stated that "all the Hitlerite intelligence is based on Brasol's (Ford's employee) and other 'documents' gathered through the medium of Mr. Ernest G. Liebold, Henry Ford's general secretary."[12]

The *Eternal Jew* (the translated German title of Ford's *International Jew*) was accepted throughout the ethnic German areas of Europe not just because of the industrialist's stature and pro-German attitude, but because his propaganda spoke directly to two of their greatest concerns in the early 1920s—German defeat in the Great War and the threat of Bolshevism.

Article after article in the *Dearborn Independent* reprinted in the *Eternal Jew* pointed out Germany as a prime example of subjugation to Jewish control and intrigue. The second anti-Semitic article in the paper, in fact, claimed that the collapse of the German economy, the armistice, and the revolution which prevented Germany from recovery all were the result of the world Jewish conspiracy. The article further claimed that during the war German Jews "were not German patriots"—that they refused to fight for their country.

The Treaty of Versailles was resented by most Germans and ardently attacked by the *Dearborn Independent*. The treaty, according to Ford's newspaper, was a Jew-inspired document designed to punish the German people and give the Jewish banking interests opportunities to continue domination. The *Independent* claimed "there were so many Jews in the German delegation that it was known by the term *kosher*."[13]

"Jew bankers," then, had started the war, sabotaged it by not fighting for their country, then arranged the peace treaty to their own ends. Here was an explanation of Germany's troubles which could relieve the people of the burden of responsibility. It was the bankers' doing, Ford said. The fact that of the 9 million Jews in Europe, more than 6 million lived in abject poverty in Poland, Russia, and the Balkans, had nothing to do with the conclusion. All Jews somehow were indicted as money changers and destroyers of German nationalism.

"Germany and Russia were the two countries scheduled for punishment by the international Jewish bankers," the *Dearborn Independent* claimed, "because these two countries were most aware of the Jew." The technique was different, but the end the same: "The professional financiers wrecked Germany. The professional reformers wrecked Russia."[14]

The Bolshevik scare in Germany after World War I was an especially emotional one. The Germans were disarmed. Unable to defend themselves, they expected invasion from Russia at any moment. Bolshevism was equated with a Jewish uprising, and everywhere stories of Jewish terrorism—murdering Germans, raping their women, killing priests on the doorsteps of their churches, and using their children for ritual blood sacrifices— were commonly heard. Joachim Fest recalls in his book *Hitler* that anti-Semites hissed of the "dreadful times in which Christian-hating, circumcized Asiatics everywhere are raising their bloodstained hands to strangle us in droves."[15]

Ford's *Dearborn Independent* encouraged these groundless

fears by linking the worldwide Communist movement to the Jews. Karl Marx, of course, was the grandson of a rabbi. Trotsky was a Jew by the name of Bronstein from St. Louis, Missouri, and while Lenin was not of Jewish blood (the *Dearborn Independent* cast doubt on that), he was married to a Jewess, which made him a gentile front for the Jews. The fact that there were enough Jews in the early Bolshevik revolution to point a finger at gave Ford's propagandists all the ammunition they needed to state emphatically that all Communists were Jews or controlled by Jews. The central group of Red philosophers on every campus were Jews as well, the *Dearborn Independent* flatly concluded.

Again, the facts did not back up the Ford claims. While there had been Bolshevik Jews, there had been far more Jewish Mensheviks, the bitter opponents of the Bolsheviks. Only 2.6 percent of the Jewish population enrolled in the Communist party in Russia in 1918. And in Germany not a single Jewish officeholder had ever been associated with the Communist party.[16] There were, of course, a few radical Marxists during this period in Germany who were Jewish. Rosa Luxemburg, a Polish Jew, was eventually imprisoned for her Bolshevik-leaning propaganda in pamphlets and books. Yet she and those like her were in a decided minority among the generally conservative German-Jewish population. The German people, however, were frightened and in no mood to listen to such reasoning. Ford's publication presented the "fact" that all Reds were Jews, and many Germans bought it.

Ford, then, spoke directly to the Germans and their emotions. He offered them a reason for their plight and implied a solution. The *International Jew* presented a letter supposedly written by a Russian patriot just after the Bolshevik revolution, stating:

"Imagine for a moment that there were no Semites in Europe. Would the tragedy be so terrible, now? Hardly! They have stirred up the people in all countries, have incited them to war, revolution, and Communism. They believe in the saying that 'there is good fishing in troubled waters.' "[17] It takes no imagination to read into this fantasy the precursor of Hitler's "final solution."

Ford's *Eternal Jew* became the first bible of the postwar anti-Semitic movement in Germany. Hammer Verlag, the notorious anti-Semitic publishing house headed by Theodore Fritsch, printed six editions of the *Eternal Jew* between 1920 and 1922. In 1923, a *Chicago Tribune* correspondent in Germany reported that Hitler's Munich organization was "sending out Mr. Ford's books . . . by the carload."[18] And by 1933, Fritsch was reportedly in the ninteenth printing of the book.[19] Later German editions presented the names Henry Ford and Adolf Hitler side by side on the cover. Other Fascist organizations, such as the World Service, printed and distributed additional editions of the book in Europe, North America, and South America.[20] While there is no way to determine how many copies were actually circulated in Germany, conservative estimates range in the millions.

The *Dearborn Independent* cooperated by referring German-speaking customers for the book to the right publisher. Liebold replied to one inquiry: "The *International Jew* may be obtained from HammerVerlag (Th. Fritsch) Leipzig. As we have given our entire attention to the problem in the United States, we are not contemplating the publication of this book in foreign languages, preferring to leave this to the people of the respective countries where such would be of benefit to them."[21]

Liebold, in a classic understatement, wrote in his reminiscences that "I do think that the publication of the *International Jew* had quite an influence in Germany."[22] Others made it clearer just how much influence the book had. Hitler youth leader Baldur von Schirach was a telling spokesman. He was a romantic with strong American ties—his mother was born in the United States and his grandfather had lost a leg as a Union soldier at Bull Run. At the Nuremburg War Crimes Trials, von Schirach testified that he had been prejudiced against the Jews at the age of seventeen by Ford's publication and that it had been a central indoctrination tool for many years within the Hitler youth movement. He added: "The younger generation looked with envy to the symbol of success and prosperity like Henry Ford, and if he said the Jews were to blame, why naturally we believed him. . . . You have no idea what a great influence this book had on the thinking of German youth."[23]

To a fledgling would-be dictator there is nothing more inspiring than money, and there are numerous indications that Henry Ford may have helped Hitler in this vital way as well. The *Manchester Guardian* reported in 1922 that Hitler received "more than merely moral support" from an American who sympathized with anti-Semitism.[24] *The New York Times* that same year reported that the Weimar government more than suspected that Ford was financing Hitler. The *Times* agreed that Hitler had to be obtaining money from some foreign source because German financial support could not possibly cover the immense expenditures that his personal and business establishment required.[25]

Hitler himself denied in a court of law in 1930 that he received money from Henry Ford.[26] Yet, as James and Suzanne Pool point out in their excellent book *Who Financed Hitler?*, for Hitler to do anything but deny it would have been foolish. Hitler could not run the risk of being seen as the "puppet of a foreign capitalist."[27]

Ford neither addressed the subject directly nor ever admitted contributing to Hitler. But he certainly had reason to do so. The most obvious motivation was to encourage the spread of his personal anti-Semitism. The Nazi party certainly could accomplish that with his money. Even more fundamental, Ford wanted to build an automobile plant in Germany. He was stopped, however, by the terms of the Versailles Treaty. If he financed Hitler, then when he came to power, the Versailles Treaty might be circumvented and the factory built. As it turned out, Hitler did set aside the treaty and Ford got his plant.

Ford not only had the motive, he also had the means to make large contributions without detection. Ford owned his company and thus had to account to no stockholders or directors for his expenditures. And Ford kept a great deal of cash on hand for any personal expenses or gifts. His large private office safe often contained upward of $1 million in cash. When his personal secretary left the company in 1944, for example, he accounted for $1.7 million in Ford's vault.[28]

Some, like novelist and union sympathizer Upton Sinclair, came right out and stated that Ford made contributions. Sinclair said Ford had spent $40,000 initially to finance reprints of the *International Jew* into German, and later Ford sent $300,000 to Hitler for the National Socialist cause.[29] Sinclair, unfortunately, never offered proof of his claim.

Officials in the U.S. government dropped hints of such contributions. William E. Dodd, U.S. Ambassador to Germany at the time, told reporters that "certain American industrialists had a great deal to do with bringing fascist regimes into being in both Germany and Italy."[30] And a major German newspaper, the *Berliner Tageblatt*, expressed its concern during the Weimar period and asked that Ambassador Alanson Houghton investigate the contributions and put a stop to them. The clearest indictment of financial aid came from the vice-president of the Bavarian Diet in a report to the President of Germany in 1922. He said:

> The Bavarian Diet has long had the information that the Hitler movement was partly financed by an American anti-Semitic who is Henry Ford. Mr. Ford's interest in the Bavarian anti-Semitic movement began a year ago when one of Mr. Ford's agents, seeking to sell tractors, came in contact with Dietrich Eckart, the notorious Pan German; shortly after, Herr Eckart asked Mr. Ford's agent for financial aid. The agent returned to America and immediately Mr. Ford's money began coming to Munich. Herr Hitler openly boasts of Mr. Ford's support and praises Mr. Ford as a great individualist and great anti-Semite.[31]

Historians generally have contended Ford did contribute to Nazism. Father Francis Charles, professor at the Jesuit College in Louvain, Belgium, maintains that Ford did finance distribution of the *International Jew* in Europe.[32] One of the most perceptive biographers of Hitler's early years, Konrad Heiden, maintains in his book *Hitler: A Biography* that the fact that Ford "gave money to the National Socialists, directly or indirectly, has never been disputed."[33] That, however, is not exactly correct.

Kurt G. W. Lüdecke, in his biography *I Knew Hitler*, denies that Ford made contributions. Lüdecke says that he visited Ford in Dearborn during his tour of the United States in 1921 to collect support for Hitler. Ford was supportive of the anti-Semitic ideas Lüdecke expressed, but did not give him any money. "If I had been trying to sell Mr. Ford wooden nutmegs," Lüdecke wrote, "he couldn't have shown less interest in the proposition. With consummate Yankee skill, he lifted the discussion back to the idealistic plane."[34]

Lüdecke, however, is less than a credible witness. Heiden asserted that Hitler could have been accused of perjury when he denied having received contributions from Ford, had "a certain witness not been too frightened to produce the incriminating documents."[35] That witness was Lüdecke. There is also evidence that when he wrote his book about his affiliation with Hitler, the year being 1937, Lüdecke was still too accessible to Nazi revenge to speak the entire truth. Lüdecke was deep in Nazi propaganda work in America, having served as secretary to the German-American Bund and the German-American Business League, which was clearly Nazi-directed. In 1942, Lüdecke was sentenced to five years in an American prison for conspiring to obstruct the Selective Service Act. He was hardly an objective source.

One of the most disputed aspects of Ford's probable contributions is not *if* he sent money to Hitler, but by what emissary. The possibilities are numerous. Sinclair said money was sent through the grandson of the ex-kaiser. That would be Prince Louis Ferdinand, whom Henry Ford befriended and gave several jobs within the company. Ferdinand, who for a time was pro-Nazi, did make visits to Hitler representing Henry Ford. Yet even Ford's personal secretary, Ernest Liebold, could have made cash deliveries on his business tours through Germany for Ford.

One of the most interesting possibilities as an emissary is Anton Lang. A native of the Bavarian town of Oberammergau, Lang played Christus in that village's world-famous passion play in 1900, 1910, and 1921. The play, a reenactment of Jesus Christ's last days on earth, had been held in the mountain village approximately every ten years since 1633. The Oberammergau passion play was notoriously anti-Semitic. The American Jewish Committee has called it "fundamentally hostile to Jews and Judaism," and a group of Christian scholars as late as the early 1970s said it "reveals the sin of anti-Semitism." The prologue of the play calls the Jews a "furious, blind people."[36] Anton Lang brought the play to America for the first time in 1923. He and his fellow villagers were in desperate financial straits during the economic chaos that followed World War I, and saw the American tour as a means to raise funds. Lang and Henry Ford met on the 1923 visit and became close friends. The Ford archives hold a great deal of correspondence between these two men during the 1920s and early 1930s. Lang is known to have made his last American tour in 1929. (Ironically, he was brought to the United States that year by producer Morris Gest, a Jew who would sue Ford in the mid-twenties because of slanderous attacks in the *Dearborn Independent*.) Henry Ford returned the visit in 1930, traveling to Oberammergau to see the play. In that year, Anton Lang, who gained fame because he looked remarkably like Leonardo da Vinci's image of Christ, gave the prologue while a younger man, Alois Lang, played Christus. Ford was so impressed by the performance that he gave young Alois a new car.[37] It is quite possible that Ford made contributions to Hitler through Anton Lang or other members of the Passion Play cast.

The Pools narrow their suspected emissaries down to two.[38] The first is Boris Brasol, the Russian who delivered the *Protocols* into Henry Ford's hands. Brasol did go to Germany during this period. Brasol is certainly a likely candidate, since, as the Pools point out, "he collaborated in Nazi intrigues on three continents." Connected to Brasol was Grand Duchess Victoria Vladimirovich, wife of the first cousin of Tsar Nicholas II. Lüdecke was given a letter of introduction from Brasol and visited her in

Nice, France. She was, by his accounts, flat broke, yet between 1922 and 1924 was said to have given more than half a million gold marks to the Nazi cause.

The second suspected courier the Pools identify is Warren "Fuzzy" Anderson, Ford's European sales manager. It was Anderson who met with Dietrich Eckart and whom the Bavarian Diet official claimed was approached for money while attempting to sell tractors. Anderson objected to Ford's anti-Semitic propaganda in Europe on the purely business grounds that it hurt sales. Ford recalled him from Europe and fired him because of the opposition, but the Pools suggest that, until his firing, Anderson could well have served as the money conduit.

The question of whether Henry Ford financially supported Hitler, and how, may never be answered completely. The evidence, if it ever existed, either no longer exists or remains hidden. Yet enough credible sources express belief and cite plausible reasons to indicate that such contributions were highly likely.

While it may not be clear if he gave money, Ford certainly lent Hitler a philosophical framework for the latter's already ardent anti-Semitism. Hitler's philosophy did not harden until the prison term for treason that he served following his 1923 Munich *putsch*. Until then, his ideology was in flux, even mirroring for a while a primitive version of Bismarck's nationalist views.[39] In a country-clublike setting at Landsberg am Lech Prison, Hitler's vision crystalized, and he wrote—or, rather, dictated to fellow prisoner Rudolf Hess—the book which would help him into national prominence. The book, of course, was *Mein Kampf* (My Struggle), and it would ultimately sell more than 10 million copies.

There is little question that Hitler had both Ford and his philosophies in mind while writing *Mein Kampf*. Dietrich Eckart tells us as much in his memoirs, published in 1924.[40] Eckart was an obscure German journalist and poet, but, more important, he was Adolph Hitler's closest friend during the Nazi development years preceding the *putsch*. Hitler, in fact, dedicates *Mein Kampf* to Eckart, who died in the 1923 struggle. Eckart's book, which traces the Jewish conspiracy to undermine civilization all the way back to Moses and the Egyptian bondage, contains references to Ford's *Eternal Jew* for much of its "factual" backgrounding.

An interesting side development during Hitler's imprisonment also underlines Ford's influence on the Nazi leader's thinking at the time. It was in Landsberg that Hitler developed the concept of the Volkswagen (People's Car).[41] The car's design copied many aspects of Ford's Model T. The Volkswagen would be a basic vehicle which any owner could repair with basic tools. It would be plain-looking yet, because of its simplicity, would generate true devotion among its owners. Best of all, it would be inexpensive, at 990 marks—$395, which is the average price Ford's Model T achieved in its heyday. Hitler promised to even outstrip Ford's production, achieving 1½ million vehicles a year at his equivalent of Ford's Dearborn Rouge complex. Later, Hitler would send the car's designer, Ferdinand Porsche, to the Rouge plant to copy Ford's manufacturing techniques.[42]

When Henry Ford sent a delegate to Germany some years later, Hitler said, "You can tell Herr Ford that I am a great admirer of his. . . . I shall do my best to put his theory into practice in Germany, which is still very backward as far as motorization goes."[43] Hitler never actually delivered Volkswagens to German workers, preferring to build war machinery instead, but the episode nonetheless says a great deal about Ford's influence on the Führer's thinking.

A more direct proof of influence is that Henry Ford is the only American mentioned in the text of *Mein Kampf*. The reference was to the struggle in America against Jewish bankers and unionists. Hitler wrote: "Every year makes them more and more the controlling masters of the producers in a nation of one hundred and twenty millions; only a single great man, Ford, to their fury still maintains full independence."[44]

The connection between Hitler's *Mein Kampf* and Henry Ford's *International Jew* is blatantly clear. Hitler plagiarized from Ford, lifting his reasoning and sometimes the very words which appeared in the *Dearborn Independent*.

Both Ford and Hitler began by placing the issue squarely in what they called "racial" context. *Dearborn Independent* articles stressed repeatedly that the Jew cannot hide behind freedom of religion because the question "is one of race and nationality." Hitler echoed this conviction, writing in *Mein Kampf* that the primary evil is in "the first and fundamental lie, the purpose of which is to make people believe that Jewry is not a nation but a religion." Both stated that these were not people of a different religion, but "an entirely different race."

Jewry was a race they said, clearly defined and inferior to the Nordic strains that both Ford and Hitler identified as superior. Ford's publications speak of the Anglo-Saxon character which "made our race great." Anglo-Saxons were the achievers, explorers, builders of civilization. The final article appearing in the *International Jew* maintains that "the only union that can be expected is a union of the superior strain." Hitler says it more bluntly in *Mein Kampf*: "Whenever Aryans have mingled their blood with that of an inferior race, the result has been the downfall of the people who were the standard-bearers of a higher civilization."

59

Within the superior race it was manifest that some would be superior to others; therefore, democracy for Ford and Hitler was repugnant. "Because there are few men of great ability," Ford said, "it is possible for a mass of men with small ability to pull the greater ones down—but in so doing they pull themselves down." On another occasion he stated that there was "no greater absurdity and no greater disservice to humanity in general than to insist that all men are equal." Hitler echoed: "Men are not of equal value or of equal importance." And, again: "The absurd notion that men of genius are born out of universal suffrage cannot be too strongly repudiated," which appears to duplicate Ford's thought that democracy is no more than a "leveling down of ability."

Both men expressed the fear that the Jew was taking over and defiling their respective soil. The *Independent* wrote that "it is necessary for industry [i.e., Jewish interests] to deplete the land both of laborers and capital." And Hitler said, "The cup is filled to overflowing when he [the Jew] draws also the land and the soil into the circle of his mercenary objects." Ford was well noted for his reverence of the farmer, and Hitler chimed in in *Mein Kampf*: "In the open country there could be no social problem, because the master and the farmhand were doing the same kind of work and doing it together. They ate their food in common, and sometimes even out of the same dish." Jews were, in both publications, a threat to this fundamentally wholesome agrarianism. In virtually identical words they wrote: "He himself never cultivated the soil but considered it as an object to be exploited."

We have already seen how Ford was reacting to the moral decay of postwar America, a decadence he saw as fostered by the influx of Jews and their influence upon the country's Anglo-Saxon society. On this point, too, Hitler took his stand in *Mein*

Kampf, declaiming on the Jews' part in prostitution and corruption of the theater and arts. On the theater, for example, Ford's publication called it "part of the Jewish program to guide public tastes," and Hitler called Jewish dominance of the theater "infection." The words are different; the thoughts are identical.

Jews, as they saw them, were corruptors and parasites on the gentile society. "If New York could be isolated," Ford's *International Jew* said, "Jewish initiative would not suffice to provide enough potatoes for the inhabitants"; to which *Mein Kampf* added, "If the Jews were the only people in the world, they would be wallowing in filth and mire and would exploit one another and try to exterminate one another in a bitter struggle."

Somehow these Jewish spoilers were gifted with superior ability, a fact both Ford and Hitler admitted. Their mastery of debate frustrated Hitler and Ford, both accusing the Jew of using language "for the purpose of dissimulating his thought, or at least, veiling it so that the real can not be discovered by what he says but rather by reading between the lines."

Yet the Jew's ability was forever committed to diabolical ends. The *Dearborn Independent* repeatedly stated that whenever Jews got a foothold, they would undermine Christian society, taking religion out of schools and politics. "The Jews are against the gentile scheme of things," according to Ford's propagandists. Hitler chimed in: "Religion is ridiculed [by Jews], customs and morality are presented as outlived." And to achieve these ends, Ford, and later Hitler, contended that Jews infiltrated and used the press, the ultimate bastion of a free society. The press was Jew-controlled, Ford maintained, and one of Germany's reasons for failure was the Jewish press. "The primary means of controlling the American people is the Jewish press," the *International Jew* contended. In *Mein Kampf,* Hitler goes into boring detail of how he was first deceived by the Jew press in Vienna. Hitler concluded, "The second weapon in the service of Jewry is the press. . . . He [the Jew] is in a position to produce and to conduct that power which under the name of public opinion is better known today than it was a few decades ago."

Hitler reiterated Ford's conclusion that Bolshevism and Judaism were synonyms. "The real organizer of the revolution," Hitler stated, "and the actual wire-puller behind it, the international Jew, had sized up the situation correctly." Later he wrote, "In Russian Bolshevism we must see Jewry's twentieth-century effort to take world domination unto itself."

Communism and unionism were all part of the same plot, according to Ford, and then Hitler. In his autobiography, *My Life and Work*, Ford said, "There seems to be a determined effort to fasten the Bolshevik stain on American labor. . . . Workingmen are made the tools of some manipulator who seeks his own ends through them." And on another occasion: "A union is a neat thing for a Jew to have on hand when he comes around to get his clutches on an industry." In *Mein Kampf*, Hitler wrote of the Jews menacing the New World through American unions. He pointed to Freemasons, as Ford did, as the Jews' original infiltration point. Hitler told a story to illustrate his point: "While Moses Cohn, stockholder, stiffened the back of his company until it became as stern and uncompromising as possible toward the demands of its workers, his brother, Isaac Cohn, labor leader, would be in the courtyard of the factory rousing the workers. 'Look at them,' Isaac would cry out, 'they only seek to crush you. Throw your chains away.' Both Isaac and Moses (who would quickly sell his stock, secretly being aware of the coming strike) would eventually profit from the collapse of the gentile company which they could then take over."

The ultimate genius of the Jew, Ford repeatedly contended, was in finance. "The whole science of economics, conservative and radical, capitalistic and anarchistic, is of Jewish origin." Jews, he said, invented capitalism and the gold standard, the greatest of evils. "The gold standard destroyed the government that accepted it, for it could not satisfy the demand for currency." Hitler, like Ford, had his romantic agrarian constituency as well. The Populist anticapitalists and free-money people in Germany were called by the rubric *volkisch*, but the stands of the American and German groups were remarkably similar. Hitler played to them by using Ford's formula of attacking the gold standard as part of the Jewish plot. He promised to abolish the gold standard if he came to power, a promise he never fulfilled. The naive argument that all economics stems from Jews seems to have been picked up by Hitler as well: "It was the Jews, of course, who invented the economic system of constant fluctuation and expansion that we call capitalism—that invention of genius, with its subtle and yet simple self-acting mechanism. Let us make no mistake about it—it is an invention of genius, of the devil's own ingenuity."

The aim was always the same to Ford. The Jews were plotting to "establish a secret empire, an invisible supergovernment of the Jews." It is worth noting that Ford's publication began writing about a Jewish world conspiracy before the *Protocols of the Learned Elders of Zion* fell into his hands. Hitler followed, stating that "the final aim of the Jewish fight . . . is the economic conquest of this world."

Ford and Hitler agreed that Jews planned the world wars, then profited from them, all to further weaken gentile society for the eventual takeover. Gentiles were used. In Ford's *International Jew,* a new term is coined, *gentile front,* meaning any flawed gentile who lets himself be used, either wittingly or not, in the Jewish cause. "Gentile fronts," the *International Jew* states, are used extensively in "the financial world today to cover up the evidence of Jewish control." "Gentile front" appears frequently in *Mein Kampf*, as well; Hitler called these individuals "screens and shop-window Christians."

Both men spoke highly of the *Protocols*, even in the face of evidence that they were rank forgeries. "The only statement I care to make about the *Protocols*," Ford said, "is that they are sixteen years old, and they have fitted the world situation up to this time." When a Hitler lieutenant told the Führer that the *Protocols* could not possibly be genuine, the reply was a rhetorical, "Why not!" Vamberto Morais, in *A Short Story of Anti-Semitism*, concludes that Hitler "did not care two straws . . . whether the story was historically true. If it was not, its intrinsic truth was all the more convincing to him."[45]

The evidence is irrefutable that Ford's publications, in fact, contributed to Adolf Hitler's magnum opus. Yet we must not assume that Hitler's philosophy was entirely stamped out in Dearborn. Although there are strong parallels in the *International Jew* and *Mein Kampf,* they both relate to a vast body of previous and contemporary anti-Semitic material upon which both leaned. Ford and Hitler drew much of their poison from the same wells. The *Protocols of the Learned Elders of Zion,* for example, was used directly by both men, and Hitler relied upon the theories of Georges Vacher de Lapouge, Ludwig Gumplowicz, Otto Ammon, and Madison Grant, whose writings must also have been uncovered by Ford's army of researchers and detectives. While he was in Vienna, the magazine *Ostara*, named after a Germanic goddess, drew Hitler's attention. It proclaimed the doctrine of Aryan purity, and Hitler sought out and studied under its editor, a defrocked priest named Jorg Lanz von Liebenfels.

It would be unfair to draw too many parallels between the personalities of Ford and Hitler even though their philosophies often showed a remarkably common orientation. The similarities are engaging and they are numerous. Neither man smoked or drank. They leaned toward vegetarianism. Both had unusually strong attachments to their mothers and were distant with their fathers. Both kept their pasts private, creating a mythical background for themselves through their own select propaganda. Ford's disputed story that his father blocked his personal development, for instance, is paralleled by Hitler's story that his father tried to push him into the Hapsburg civil service against his wishes, an allegation historians have disputed.

Both would learn to eliminate their opposition. The method used, however, represents a fundamental difference between Hitler and Henry Ford. Ford would have them fired; Hitler had them murdered. Father Staempfle, a priest who edited *Mein Kampf* and thus got too close to Hitler, for instance, was exterminated by one of Hitler's special death squads because he knew too much. Ford, on the other hand, was a pacifist in these early years. Here was a fundamental, and profound difference. Had Ford actually read *Mein Kampf,* he would have seen Hitler's statement that "the pacifist-humanitarian idea may indeed become an excellent one when the most superior type of manhood will have succeeded in subjugating the world to such an extent that this type is then sole master of the earth. . . . So first of all, the fight and then pacifism." Violence was, from the very outset, fundamental to Hitler's fascism. Even before *Mein Kampf,* Hitler's storm troopers were raiding union halls and Jewish places of business. Between 1923 and 1931 some forty

synagogues and more than 100 Jewish cemeteries were dese-
crated, largely by the Nazis.[46] Ford's *International Jew*, for all its
hatred, did not once advocate such violence, but patiently
insisted on rational discussion to resolve what Ford saw as the
world's Jewish problem.

The importance of Ford's *International Jew* in the rise of
Hitler lies mainly in contributing thoroughly professional
propaganda material for the growing Nazi movement. Like a
two-act moral drama, the German people were first presented
with the "facts" by a world folk hero and humanitarian industrialist, then they sat through Hitler's duplicate performance.
The play was emotionally convincing, and to desperate Germans seeking answers to postwar confusion and fear, any big lie
became plausible.

4

Ford
Re-Tractor
•

For two years Ford's newspaper remained virtually silent on "the Jewish question," slipping only occasionally to include a vindictive line about bankers or Hollywood producers. Ford was busy elsewhere then trying to buy several incomplete dams in Muscle Shoals, Alabama—dams we know today as the Tennessee Valley Authority.

The federal government simply did not have the money or desire to finish the Muscle Shoals projects at the time. Ford offered to buy the nitrate plants around the incomplete Wilson Dam for 5 million dollars and to lease the dam itself for 100 years. Ford wanted the plants to produce nitrate fertilizer; that would fit nicely into his tractor and implement business. He and his friend Thomas Edison were obsessed with the idea that water power was the energy of the future, and Ford wanted to experiment with it. His vision incorporated the creation of a series of small communities along the river, each supplying the work force for a single nitrate plant, and where the part-time farmers could gain the benefits of industrialization without having to live in wicked cities. The Muscle Shoals project meant a great deal to Ford. In fact, he told one biographer that he would rather have that project than another billion dollars.

Congress did not accept Ford's offer. It was ridiculously low and seemed to many of the legislators completely one-sided. One congressman called it the "most wonderful real estate speculation since Adam and Eve lost title to the Garden of Eden." A four-year-long political battle ensued between Ford's forces and his congressional opposition, led by Senator George Norris of Nebraska. During that time, Ford set out to woo the farmers, who, he felt, could give him the support needed to get his Muscle Shoals deal approved by Congress.[1] To that end, he made several trips to the project area, taking Edison along, and promised prosperity to the farmers of the valley. With just a few words from Ford, developers crowded into the rural community. They founded an entire town called Highland Park, paved streets through cornfields, and gave them familiar Detroit street names such as John R and Woodward. Ford stirred up the farmers as much as he could, convincing them that only the greedy nitrate interests and Wall Street (both Jewish, in his litany) stood between them and prosperity.

While the battle for support raged in Congress between the Ford and Norris factions, the *Dearborn Independent* began to champion the farmers' problems, real and imagined. To further his cause, Ford's newspaper revived its favorite scapegoat—the Jews. In the spring of 1924, the *Independent* began to convince the farmers that they were victims of a Jewish conspiracy to gain complete control of their money and land.

68

JEWISH EXPLOITATION OF FARMER'S ORGANIZATIONS: MONOPOLY TRAPS OPERATE UNDER GUISE OF MARKETING ASSOCIATIONS, the first headline in the series announced on April 23. The introductory sentence summed up the idea for the entire campaign: "A band of Jews—bankers, lawyers, moneylenders, advertising agencies, fruitpackers, produce buyers, professional office managers, and bookkeeping experts—is on the back of the American farmer." The technique the "conspirators" ostensibly used was to sow the seeds of dissatisfaction with existing marketing techniques and "local" cooperatives, then step in with a high-powered business person who would promise far better returns for their crops. The Jews would thus gain control and drain funds from the farmer, holding him in check with binding contracts. Next, the Jews would combine all the various cooperative associations in the United States and the world. Thus, the new charges fit the old suit, and the Jew was again on trial in Ford's paper for conspiring for world domination.[2]

The attack conformed to another of Ford's deep-seated prejudices against any kind of workers' organization. He saw the farmer as an individualist and ignored the fact that typically he was already being exploited by a single buyer who dictated crop prices. "I don't believe in cooperation," Ford said to a magazine reporter. "What can cooperation do for farmers? All it amounts to is an attempt to raise the price of farm products. It defeats its own purpose because if prices go too high, people won't buy."[3]

Farmers wrote in by the hundreds encouraging the *Dearborn Independent*'s new crusade, not so much because they were against cooperatives but because they disliked Jews. Reading through the *Dearborn Indepedent* correspondence is a disheartening education in bigotry. "The dirty devils of Jews should be run out of the country," one letter said. "The Bible says Jews will return to Palestine, but they want to get all the money out of America first," wrote another. The hostility from farmers, most of whom had probably never met a Jew, was remarkable. It reflected the paranoia of the isolated farm life, a preoccupation with a perceived persecution by bankers, city people, and foreigners with which Ford's newspaper was quick to sympathize.[4]

Looking for Jewish plots behind the cooperative movement, Ford's newspaper brought up again all of the names it had criticized in the past. Such eminent Jewish Americans as Bernard Baruch, Otto Kahn, Albert Lasker, Eugene Meyer, and Julius Rosenwald were once more targeted as conspirators in the co-op takeover plot. At the head of this distinguished group, the *Independent* named Aaron Sapiro, a prominent Chicago attorney and cooperative organizer.

Sapiro was a colorful and volatile figure in the cooperative movement. He had gained national recognition and respect by organizing tobacco and cotton growers in the South, fruit growers in California, potato growers in Maine, and wheat farmers in Canada. Numerous organizations, including the National Council of Farmers' Cooperative Marketing Associations, endorsed him and protested Ford's attacks. Sapiro believed firmly that a market cooperative representing in the market all of the producers of a single crop was the only way to increase the farmer's profits.

Sapiro inspired controversy as well as a large entourage of supporters. He was aggressive to the point of violence at times, often dictatorial with cooperative members and managers, and known for his personal conceit. His fees for services were high, but probably no more so than those of the best lawyer in any specialized field: "I am not interested in money," Sapiro said, "I am interested in raising the standards of living of the farmers. I am interested in pulling the children out of the cotton field and placing them in schools; in pulling the women out of the cotton fields and placing them in homes."[5]

When the *Dearborn Independent* attacked his leadership and character as well as his entire movement, Sapiro filed a $1 million libel suit aimed not at the newspaper but at its owner, Henry Ford. The *Dearborn Independent* said they welcomed the lawsuit. It would further expose Sapiro's system, which, they contended, was their only goal. "In a court of law that system can be turned, even to its inmost corners, to the bright light of competent and impartial scrutiny."[6]

The Jewish community was less enthusiastic about such a court battle. American Jewish Committee President Louis Marshall contended, "It gives Ford the publicity which he has craved ever since he embarked upon his attack [on] the Jews."[7] Both sides were right about the publicity, for the Sapiro-Ford trial became one of the most thoroughly publicized suits of its day, grabbing front-page coverage in such prestigious newspapers as *The New York Times* and the *Chicago Tribune*.

In the Ford camp, the decision was made to make this a major battle. For the two years between the time the suit was filed and the case actually came to trial in March 1927, Ford sent his team of detectives and lawyers across the country to gain any shred of evidence against Sapiro, virtually retracing every one of his steps over the previous twelve years. In the process they amassed 125 witness affidavits and more than 40,000 pages of depositions.[8] Ford hired six of the best trial lawyers, led by U.S. Senator James A. Reed of Missouri and the company lawyer Clifford Longley. Reed alone received $100,000 for his services.[9]

From the first day of the trial, it was also apparent that Ford's detective force would be in full operation in and around the

71

courtroom. Fifty Ford detectives all but blocked traffic in the Federal Building.[10] Later, Sapiro's lawyer would complain, "Ford agents had made a practice of tapping telephone wires, wiring the private rooms of various persons and even the chambers of judges, examining private letters and private baggage, employing neighborhood merchants to spread propaganda, going into the homes of jurors posing as salesmen, sending notes of warning to jurors, and doing many other things of the kind."[11]

Sapiro's defense staff was modest by comparison. He had decided to finance it alone, neither asking for nor accepting any support from Jewish organizations naturally concerned about the anti-Semitic implications of the case. Sapiro, however, did offer one surprise. Instead of the "Jew lawyer from New York" Ford's staff expected to defend Sapiro, he brought in William Henry Gallagher, an Irish Catholic lawyer with an outstanding record in Detroit courts.[12] Strategically, the choice was brilliant, for Gallagher, operating on his home turf, proved a match for the oration of the white-haired senator from Kansas City.

Senator Reed's first move in the case was to request that all reference in the trial to Jews be avoided. He obviously wanted to sidestep defending Ford's anti-Semitism, so blatantly presented in the series of twenty *Dearborn Independent* articles. Gallagher protested, "There is no use in trying to pull the wool over our eyes and tell ourselves this is only an attack on Aaron Sapiro."[13] But Reed had the point of law on his side. The Jewish people were not bringing the suit, would receive no damage settlements, and therefore could not be at issue in the case. The judge had no choice but to agree with Reed's argument and ban any such reference from being presented to the jurors.

William Cameron, Ford's editor, next took the stand and

stunned everyone by taking full blame for the entire series and every statement in it. Mr. Ford, Cameron claimed, had not authorized the articles, had never read them, and, until the suit was filed, had never even heard of Aaron Sapiro. The boss never read his own paper, Cameron insisted. One Ford biographer, William Richards, noted that "no one ever got around to ask if some of the articles in proof were read to him,"[14] a comment made only half tongue in cheek, since Cameron was known for reading his best lines aloud as Ford sat by slouched in a chair.

The strategy of shifting the blame away from Ford had been developing for some time. During the first series of articles against the Jews, for example, Ernest Liebold explained the position to a complaining dealer: "So long as Mr. Ford personally keeps out of it, I am confident that it can be brought to a successful end." He added that this would leave Ford "free to take whatever action he chooses."[15]

In the courtroom, however, the ploy of laying it all on Cameron was, at best, ridiculous. The *Dearborn Independent* was promoted as "Ford's Own Paper," and statements coming from Liebold and Cameron were marked "Authorized by Henry Ford." In his reminiscences, Liebold admits everything was being done against the Jews because of Ford's wishes.[16] The argument was pierced during the trial when James Martin Miller, a former *Dearborn Independent* employee, testified that Ford had said, "He [Sapiro] was organizing the farmers with the bunch of Jews down there, and trying to bilk them."[17] The Ford crew, however, continued to maintain his complete innocence in the matter throughout the trial. Miller later wrote to Samuel Untermeyer, stating: "I wrote a book about Ford, unfortunately; sent to do it by book publishers in heat of the Ford presidential talk. I tell about his anti-Jew propaganda, quoting him in that book. I was with him a very great deal. Ford personally knew all about the attack on the Jews made in the *Dearborn Independent*. I never had a visit with him, at lunch or dinner, when he did not talk about the Jews and his campaign against them."[18]

As the trial unfolded, it became more and more apparent that Aaron Sapiro was proving his libel case. The Ford lawyers had little to substantiate the *Dearborn Independent*'s printed charges. Sapiro apparently had oversold the benefits of his program to farmers at the time and used high-pressure techniques to encourage farmers to join up. He held farmers to their contracts, even suing several of them for breach of contract. But these offenses were insignificant compared to the criticisms of Sapiro's operation in the *Dearborn Independent*. The Ford defense shifted more and more to proving that Sapiro was overpaid for his services. Sapiro received $30,000 for a three-week campaign in which he delivered eight speeches for the Tobacco Growers Cooperative. His retainer's fee for eight months' work on behalf of the tobacco growers amounted to $22,845.[19] Since Sapiro's services included his legal staff's efforts as well, the large sums mentioned raised few eyebrows. The case droned on, going into minute detail on financial points and keeping Sapiro on the witness stand for seven days. Reporters were half asleep, and the stories they published on this segment of the trial did the same for readers tenacious enough to follow the case. When Sapiro's cross-examination was over, the reporters began to ask if Henry Ford would actually take the witness stand.

Ford had no desire to appear. He avoided being served with a subpoena for some time. Finally, a young lawyer posed as a newsman to get near Ford. Edsel had brought his father that day to the Ford Airport for a celebration, and Ford was sitting in a Lincoln convertible watching a plane take off when the lawyer dropped the subpoena and a five-dollar bill for the witness fee in Ford's lap. "No, no," Ford yelled, "take it away." The lawyer then turned and ran, but was soon apprehended by Ford's body-guards who claimed that it was not Henry Ford the lawyer had served with a subpoena but Ford's brother John. Hoping to get away without broken bones, the young lawyer said, "Then what's all the fuss about?" During the trial, Ford's lawyers argued that the subpoena had not been served properly because it fell between Ford's knees and onto the floor. Gallagher said in that case Ford should be charged with contempt of court, and the Ford lawyers backed down, agreeing that Ford would come forward on his own. He was to appear on April Fool's Day.[20] The last time he had been on the witness stand he had made a complete fool of himself, and reporters couldn't believe he would give his opposition another chance at him. They were right.

On a Sunday evening, the day before he was to testify, Ford was injured in an automobile crash. He had left his mansion, Fair Lane, that day, driving alone in a Model T coupe, to visit his engineering laboratory in Highland Park. Late the evening Ford appeared on foot at Fair Lane's gatehouse obviously dazed and injured. Two days later he was admitted to Ford Hospital.

His story was that after he had left home, he saw a couple of men in a Studebaker watching him. The two men leaned forward in their car and watched him with great interest. Ford had a habit of waving to passing motorists, and when he did, they waved back, but it was all very suspicious, Ford thought. As he drove back that night along Michigan Avenue, Dearborn's main street, the Studebaker sideswiped his car and went on. Ford lost control and veered off the road, over a stone curb, down a fifteen-foot embankment, and into a tree. From the position of the car, it appeared that, had it not hit the tree, it would have gone over into the Rouge River.

The story was not released to the press until Ford was actually in the hospital. Cameron's explanation for the delay in giving the news to the public was the court case and the delicate nature of the situation. But once the newspapers got the story, they unleashed a flood of yellow journalism, with headlines and stories telling of an assassination plot and that Ford was near death in the hospital. Detroiters were even informed at one point that Ford was dead. Some reports had it that the hit-and-run was committed by drunks.[21]

The Ford Motor Company issued statements dispelling any notion of foul play. Harry Bennett, the head of the Ford Rouge security force, stepped in and took charge of the investigation, working with the Dearborn Police, but a formal complaint was never filed. Bennett assured reporters there was no plot. "Our connections with the Detroit underworld are such that within twenty-four hours of the hatching of such a plot as this has been called, we would know of it. I believe this is one of those accidents that will never be solved."[22] Shortly thereafter a report was issued from the Wayne County Prosecutor's office that the identity of the two young men in the Studebaker was known, yet no action would be taken.

The accident was all too convenient for Henry Ford's purpose of staying out of court. The injuries were real enough; Ford's back and sides were bruised, and he passed a small amount of blood through the kidneys. It is unlikely that the entire medical staff of Henry Ford Hospital would have acceded to faking the reports. Yet it appears Ford may well have created the accident. Cameron soon released the statement that the accident actually had occurred, even though some people might draw certain unavoidable and unfounded inferences from the event. Until Cameron's statement, no reporter questioned the authenticity of Ford's story. After that, several reporters began checking it out. They went to the accident scene precisely at the same time of day with the same weather conditions as the official communiqué reported. The accident was supposed to have occurred on Dearborn's busiest street at a time of the evening when there were many people out and around. The reporters concluded that such an accident should have drawn a large crowd, particularly with Henry Ford at the wheel. Yet there were no witnesses, and Ford had supposedly walked home from the accident alone. Two youngsters said they had seen Ford standing beside his car just before the reported time of the accident.[23] More recently, Harry Bennett's autobiography told a new version of the accident. Bennett says that he visited the Fair Lane mansion as soon as he found out about it, and was allowed in to see Ford. Ford told him that he had not been in the car, and now they had the time to settle the Sapiro thing.[24]

Two days after admission to Ford Hospital, Ford was released to convalesce at home. Two weeks later his doctors reported to the court that he was still in no condition to testify. Attempts by Gallagher to appoint a court doctor to verify the seriousness of Ford's condition were blocked. Soon they were unnecessary, for another strange event abruptly ended the case.

Harry Bennett's espionage work had resulted in affidavits from fourteen Ford Motor Company employees testifying that Sapiro had attempted to bribe the jurors, and that one juror had accepted a package from Sapiro's people. The woman was Cara Hoffman, and Bennett zeroed in on her, also claiming that she had lied about her husband's occupation, stating he was a plumbing contractor when in fact he ran a "blind pig," an illegal drinking establishment. On the witness stand, Bennett also charged that Mrs. Hoffman had lied by saying she had no bias in the case, though she actually wanted to be assigned to the jury so she could "make it unhealthy for Old Man Ford." She had contact, the Ford detectives claimed, with J. Miller, a Detroit real estate agent who was a Jew. Since Sapiro was also a Jew, well, wasn't that proof enough they were conspiring? Mrs. Hoffman made the tactical blunder of defending herself when interviewed by a *Detroit Times* reporter. She said, "It seems to me that someone is trying to keep this case away from the jury." With that expression of bias on the record, the judge had no choice but to declare a mistrial and rescheduled the case for six months later.[25]

Now Ford had a chance to settle the matter out of the courtroom. To accomplish this, he enlisted the aid of Joseph A. Palma, a Ford dealer and former U.S. Secret Service agent, and E. J. Davis, another trusted employee. They, in turn, contacted two prominent Jews: Louis Marshall and Congressman Nathan Perlman. "I wish this wrong could be righted," Ford was said to have told Palma, urging him to do whatever was necessary to resolve the conflict between him and the Jews. Three conditions were put forth for a settlement. Ford must first publish a public apology to Sapiro. Second, he must make a statement to the press withdrawing his charges against the Jewish people. And, finally, he must fire William Cameron and Ernest Liebold, the two most notorious anti-Semites on the Ford staff. Ford added another promise, that he would change the *Dearborn Independent* into an internal company publication. Instead, he permanently shelved the periodical the following December.

Ford made the retraction. More precisely, Marshall and Perlman wrote the retraction and Ford authorized it. Actually, Ford never signed the apology or even read it. Harry Bennett

78

took the draft of the statement to Ford and told him, "It's pretty bad, Mr. Ford"; but Ford refused either to read it or have it read to him. He told Bennett, "I don't care how bad, just settle this up. The worse they make it, the better." Bennett was a master at signing Ford's signature so accurately that no one could tell the difference. Bennett signed it, delivered it to Marshall for verification, and the task was complete.[26] Marshall was amazed. He had expected Ford to use his version only as a basis for his own text, and instead he authorized it without the change of a single word. Marshall later told a friend that "if I had his money, I would not make such a humiliating statement for one hundred million dollars."[27]

Arthur Brisbane, a journalist friend of Ford's who had been critical of his anti-Semitism, held a press conference to deliver the statement on Ford's behalf.[28] He spoke warmly of Ford and added his own argument that Ford was not a racist. Brisbane recalled a statement Ford had made to him, which went as follows:

> Nobody can accuse me of being hostile to the Jewish people as a race. I employ thousands of them. They include many of my ablest associates. This building, which I believe to be the finest of its kind in the world, was built for me by Albert Kahn, Jewish architect here in Detroit, a man in my opinion with no superior.
>
> You know about the Wayside Inn which I bought in New England to perpetuate its interesting memories. I wanted to have it refurnished with authentic furniture of the correct period, tried various dealers, not Jewish, and could not get what I wanted. I then asked a Jewish dealer in Boston, Mr. Saks, to do the work for me and he has done it for me ever since, satisfactorily and honorably.
>
> I am hostile to concerns that seek to control others and make

79

money hard to get, no matter what their race or religion, but I am not hostile to Jews.

Later, Ford introduced a man who entered the room as "one of the best men that has worked with me from the beginning." This man, Brisbane said, was a Jew.

After this sterling presentation, Brisbane handed over the Ford statement. A hush must have fallen over the room as they read it in absolute astonishment. The next morning, the retraction appeared in every major newspaper in the country, in most cases word for word. It read:

> For some time past I have given consideration to the series of articles concerning Jews which since 1920 have appeared in the *Dearborn Independent.* Some of them have been reprinted in pamphlet form under the title *The International Jew.* Although public publications are my property, it goes without saying that in the multitude of my activities it has been impossible for me to devote personal attention to their management or to keep informed as to their contents. It has therefore inevitably followed that the conduct and policies of [my] publications had to be delegated to men whom I placed in charge of them and upon whom I relied implicitly.
>
> To my great regret I have learned that Jews generally, and particularly those of this country, not only resent these publications as promoting anti-Semitism, but regard me as their enemy. Trusted friends with whom I have conferred recently have assured me in all sincerity that in their opinion the character of the charges and insinuations made against the Jews, both individually and collectively, contained in many of the articles which have been circulated periodically in the *Dearborn Independent,* and have

been reprinted in the pamphlets mentioned, justifies the righteous and indignation entertained by Jews everywhere toward me because of the mental anguish occasioned by the unprovoked reflections made upon them.

This has led me to direct my personal attention to the subject, in order to ascertain the exact nature of these articles. As a result of this survey I confess I am deeply mortified that this journal, which is intended to be constructive and not destructive, has been made the medium for resurrecting exploded fictions, for giving currency to the so-called *Protocols of the Wise Men of Zion,* which have been demonstrated, as I learn, to be gross forgeries, and for contending that the Jews have been engaged in a conspiracy to control the capital and the industries of the world, besides laying at their door many offenses against decency, public order, and good morals.

Had I appreciated even the general nature, to say nothing of the details, of these utterances, I would have forbidden their circulation without a moment's hesitation. . . . I deem it my duty as an honorable man to make amends for the wrong done to the Jews as fellow-men and brothers, by asking their forgiveness for the harm that I have unintentionally committed, by retracting so far as lies within my power the offensive charges laid at their door by these publications, and by giving them the unqualified assurance that henceforth they may look to me for friendship and good will.

Ford settled with Sapiro for an estimated $140,000; the precise amount was never disclosed by either man.[29] The retraction was subsequently printed in the *Dearborn Independent.* Again, the tactic that Henry Ford knew nothing of the articles and that the writer was to blame was used, yet the retraction was clear and emphatic, stating in part that "statements as may have reflected upon Mr. Sapiro's honor or integrity, impugned his motives, or challenged the propriety of his personal or professional actions are withdrawn. Likewise the charge that there was a Jewish ring which sought to exploit the American farmer through cooperative associations is withdrawn."[30]

The third demand, to fire Cameron and Liebold, was announced in public. Yet neither man left Ford's employment. Cameron was sent to Ireland for a brief stay and given a new Lincoln, but he was soon back as Ford's official voice. Liebold was fired as manager of the *Dearborn Independent*, but kept his top position as Ford's general manager.

The retractions sent a shock wave through the Ford empire. Apparently, Ford had told Bennett to make the public statement without informing anyone, including his son Edsel. Senator Reed called from Texas to ask, "What in hell is this I see in the Dallas papers?" No one was more stunned than Cameron, who was told about the announcement by a *New York Times* reporter. Ford would not make such a statement without advising him, he protested, and insisted that he would have been the first to know. "It is all news to me," Cameron said, "and I cannot believe it is true."[31]

Reactions to Ford's 600-word retraction were, for the most part, remarkably favorable, especially in the Jewish communities. Scores of letters poured into Henry Ford's office, most of them from Jews, virtually all praising his action. Louis Marshall evoked the Jewish spirit of forgiveness, as did other prominent Jewish leaders who had so recently been slandered in the pages of the *Dearborn Independent*. The *American Hebrew* wrote that Ford's confession "must be accepted as a true repentant; it breathes honesty and sincerity no matter how the cynic may rationalize the motives behind the document. We forgive and will seek to forget." The editor of the *Jewish Tribune* said, "It is never too late to make amends and I congratulate Mr. Ford that he has at last seen the light. He will find that the spirit of forgiveness is not entirely a Christian virtue."

Even the music makers were convinced. Billy Rose, the well-known composer and theatrical producer, wrote a song entitled "Since Henry Ford Apologized to Me." It went:

> I was sad and I was blue,
> But now I'm just as good as you,
> Since Hen-ry Ford a-pol-o-gized to me.
> I've thrown a-way my lit-tle Che-vro-let
> And bought my-self a Ford Cou-pe.
> I told the Sup-'rin-ten-dent that
> The Dearborn In-de-pen-dent
> Does-n't have to hang up where it used to be.
> I'm glad he changed his point of view,
> And I even like Edsel too,
> Since Hen-ry Ford a-pol-o-gized to me.
> My mother says she'll feed him if he calls
> 'Ge-fil-te-fish' and mat-zo balls.
> And if he runs for President,
> I would-n't charge a sin-gle cent.
> I'll cast my bal-lot ab-sol-lute-ly free
> Since Hen-ry Ford a-pol-o-gized to me.[32]

During this same period, Ford took the opportunity to elimi-nate another long-pending lawsuit. New York editor Herman Bernstein had sued Ford for $1 million over the *Dearborn Inde-pendent*'s anti-Semitic articles and publication of the *Protocols*. Interestingly, in this case, too, Cameron swore he had written the piece over which Bernstein was suing Ford. "It was never called to Ford's attention," Cameron claimed in legal papers filed on the case. John Cote Dahlinger, who wrote a book claiming he is Henry Ford's illegitimate son, says Ford insisted that his articles and books had not incited pogroms in Europe, but if Bernstein could prove it, then he would apologize. While Bernstein was in Europe digging out the facts, the Sapiro case was concluded. Bernstein returned and also settled out of court. Dahlinger says Ford "also repaid Bernstein for the cost of his European trip."[33]

The general press was favorable, but not nearly as forgiving as the Jews. The *New York Telegram* said, "If one of the richest men in the world cannot get away with an anti-Semitic movement in this country, nobody else will have the nerve to try it, and of that we can all be thankful, gentiles as well as Jews." Other newspapers called Ford's actions the act of a courageous American. But a *New York Times* editorial pointed out the absurdity of Ford's claim that he was unaware, when every leader in the country had been bringing the matter to his attention for seven years. And the *New York Herald Tribune* said, "Nobody but Mr. Ford could be ignorant of a major policy of his own newspaper. Nobody but Mr. Ford could be unaware of the national and international repercussions."[34]

Adolf Hitler was told about the retraction, but ignored it. The general feeling in Germany was that Ford had been forced to apologize by international Jews, and such a retraction was meaningless.

Why Ford chose such a sweeping conclusion to his anti-Semitic crusade can only be speculated. The one answer which can be immediately rejected, in the face of Ford's actions in later years, is that he was sincerely contrite and no longer believed in the Jewish conspiracy. Political reporters suggested that Ford had again been bitten with the presidential bug and decided to go after the Jewish vote. The fear of another court trial and the possibility of having to take the stand was, of course, an inducement to settle the fight. Most observers, however, thought that Ford simply wanted to sell more cars. The Model T's life had ended, and Ford was about to bring out an entirely new car. He couldn't afford to affront any segment of the market now, especially with Chevrolet making major gains on him. Will Rogers probably said it best: "Ford used to have it in for the Jewish people until he saw them in Chevrolets, and then he said, 'Boys, I am all wrong.' "[35] An answer that is perhaps as good as any of these comes from William Richards, who pointed out the Astrologers' Guild of New York statement that Ford should no longer insult people because Jupiter and Uranus were over his Neptune, and Mercury was in his third house.[36]

On the day the retraction appeared in the *Dearborn Independent*, Henry Ford celebrated his sixty-fourth birthday. It appeared that now, at an age when most men retire, he was setting aside old prejudices and perhaps mellowing toward life. Nothing could have been further from the truth. The Sapiro trial and retraction only served to end Ford's public anti-Semitic attacks. It marked the end of his open hostility, introducing a new period in which Ford would continue to influence the course of anti-Semitism for two more decades.

5

The Friendly Puppeteer

Aᴄᴛᴇʀ his public retraction, Henry Ford appeared to be a changed man. He was, but not in the way most people perceived him then. The public saw a humbled man who genuinely wanted to make amends for the wrongs he had perpetrated against the Jewish people. To show his sincerity, he took out $150,000 worth of advertising in Jewish newspapers, the first time the Ford Motor Company had ever advertised in ethnic publications. In 1927, in fact, about 12 percent of Ford's entire advertising budget on the new Model A went into Jewish publications.[1] Ford also made appearances at the banquets of Jewish organizations and even attended testimonials for leading Jewish figures, though he never spoke at those affairs. He even managed to charm Louis Marshall, who had been so thoroughly slandered in the *Dearborn Independent*. Ford had visited Marshall's New York office on a number of occasions and offered his services in any way possible to amend for his mistakes.

87

"You have probably noticed," Marshall wrote in a letter to Herman Bernstein in 1928, "Ford is carrying out his promises in every way." But in the same letter, Marshall commented, "I was very much amused at what Henry Ford told me when he called on me some weeks ago. He said that Cameron is out of a job and had indicated his willingness to write on the Jewish side of the subject."[2] Marshall, of course, had no way of knowing how great a lie Ford had told him.

Far from being out of a job and willing to write for the Jews, Cameron was in Ford's complete grace and preparing to immediately launch a new publication with anti-Semitism as its focus. Cameron made no retraction; in fact, he told Nazi promoter Kurt Lüdecke in 1928, "It is certain that I for my part will never make a retraction. What I have written will stand. Not one thing will I take back."[3] Knowing the close relationship Cameron had with Ford, one can assume that Cameron soon expressed these views to his boss. Ford knew full well when he talked to Marshall that he had not fired Cameron and that his chief speech writer was embarking on a new publication.

Destiny was the name of the new magazine. It was the official organ of the Anglo-Saxon Federation of America, and its first president and publication editor was William Cameron. The magazine and organization both came into being within weeks after the Ford retraction. The organization embodied Cameron's long-standing belief in the ideals of the British Israelite movement, embellished with new anti-Semitic fervor. The basic premise of the "Israelites" was Aryan racial superiority. Jesus, they said, was not a Jew. And the Jews, as we know them, are not the true sons of Israel. It was the Anglo-Saxons who descended from the ten lost tribes of Israel, they claimed, while Jews descended from Judeans. The lost tribes were the good guys; the Judeans, the evil ones. Jew hating was thus justifiable, based on the long-standing "battle of righteousness" between the Aryan sons of Israel and the Jewish antagonists. Although the ridiculous theory had utterly no historical corroboration, Cameron's federation claimed that "the facts" were actually written on the great pyramids of Egypt. The fact that trained Egyptologists did not interpret the inscriptions that way only served to prove to the federation that the archeologists had been paid off by international Jews.[4]

The publications of the Anglo-Saxon Federation were blatantly anti-Semitic. *Destiny* carried on the issues familiar in the *Dearborn Independent,* including allegations of a racially motivated Jewish struggle for dominance. A series of pamphlets with anti-Semitic themes was promoted. They included such titles as "The Jewish Question," "The Servant Race," and "The Prophetic Forecast of Israel's Destiny." The author of the booklets was attributed to be an R. H., Sawyer, yet no individual by that name ever made an appearance. Sawyer's flamboyant, eloquent style was virtually identical to Cameron's, leading some to suspect they were one and the same.[5] Above all, the federation also published and distributed copies of the *Protocols of the Learned Elders of Zion.*

Cameron's involvement in the Anglo-Saxon Federation continued throughout the 1930s and won the admiration and adherence of anti-Semites and pro-Fascists. Robert Edward Edmondson, who had a reputation as a prolific Nazi propagandist, wrote to the federation, endorsing it and stating, "I am in entire sympathy with the fact that the Jews are the directive forces back of our subversive activities."[6]

Ford first ignored comments about Cameron's federation. Then, when numerous protests appeared, the federation moved its offices from Detroit to Haverhill, Massachusetts. Cameron turned over the presidency to a friend, A. F. Knoblock, but he kept the title of federation publications director.[7] When the pressure of accusations about Ford's knowledge of and consent to Cameron's activities became too great, the company issued a press release that said, "Ford Motor Company has always extended to Ford employees the fullest freedom from any coercion with respect to their views on political, religious or social activities, and they cannot be reproved by us for exercising such liberties."[8]

Ford stayed in the background when it came to fulfilling his promise of eliminating the *International Jew* from circulation. When, for example, Ford wrote to all of the book's publishers in 1928 stating that his name ought not to be used in connection with the book, he neglected to follow up his statement with action. One German publisher said he would destroy the last 9,000 copies of the *International Jew* he had in stock if Ford would pay him the modest sum of 40,000 marks. Liebold ignored the request. Thereafter, the publisher assumed Ford was not interested in stopping circulation and he not only sold out the stock in his warehouse, but went through a dozen more printings. On another occasion, a Brazilian publishing house wrote to Liebold asking for permission to publish the *International Jew*. Liebold wrote back that permission wasn't necessary, since the book was never copyrighted. He neglected to inform the publisher of Henry Ford's earlier retraction, and certainly made it appear as if the company were giving its blessing to the reprint.[9]

It took a concerted effort for Ford to ignore the continuing circulation of the *International Jew*. Many people from the Jewish community kept reminding him. Rabbi Leo Frank wrote to Liebold several times about the matter between 1933 and 1935, but received only terse replies; Frank was unable to penetrate the secretarial guardian to talk directly with Ford.[10] The Anti-Defamation League tried, too, without results. In 1936, Cameron told a reporter from the *American Hebrew* that he considered the matter of the *International Jew* closed, even though he was at that time selling digested versions of it through the federation.[11] And finally in 1937, after repeated requests by civil rights lawyer Samuel Untermeyer to make a statement, Liebold simply said that the anti-Jewish book had no connection to Ford. The book, Liebold said, "erroneously refers to Mr. Ford as its author, and steps will be taken to prevent the continued misuse of his name."[12] All attempts failed to get Ford to personally denounce the book after his initial retraction in 1927.

Ford had started the Jew-hatred snowball rolling and he was now content to stand on the sidelines and watch it grow, with only occasional, and generally covert, encouragement from him along the way. And the snowball grew. There were only five anti-Semitic organizations in the United States before 1932, including the *Dearborn Independent* and the Anglo-Saxon Federation. Between 1933 and 1940 there were no fewer than 121 separate anti-Semitic groups.[13] As Nathan Belth says in his excellent book *A Promise to Keep,* these organizations were neither political nor extremely powerful; "their unstable, alienated members were motivated more by their hates than their loyalties."[14] And for ammunition for their hate and elitism, they turned to Ford writings of the twenties, at the same time expressing respect and admiration for the industrialist. William Dudley Pelley, for example, was the head of the Silver Shirts, a pro-Nazi and anti-Semitic organization. In his publication the *Weekly Liberation,* he often praised Ford for his continuing fight "against the onslaughts of the Jewish Reds."[15]

Ford neither spoke of nor openly endorsed these groups, yet to some there appeared to be a kinship that went well beyond shared prejudice. Take, for example, Reverend Gerald Winrod of Wichita, Kansas. Winrod led a group called Defenders of the Christian Faith, a hell-and-brimstone evangelistic organization that claimed 125,000 members at its peak. He published two magazines, *The Constitutionalist* and *The Revealer*. In them, Winrod promoted the *Protocols* and followed the *Dearborn Independent* line, including implications that President Roosevelt was a Jew and that wars were Jew-inspired. He also vigorously distributed Nazi propaganda. In 1934, Winrod received a large sum of money and suddenly went to Germany for several months. When he returned, he had what for him was a new theme: Communism was a real threat, and the Jews were the real backers. No connection could be drawn between Winrod and Ford.[16] But William Cameron, Ford's voice to the nation, was reported to have been a "large donor" to Winrod's organization.[17] Cameron was a devout British Israelite who was not accustomed to donating to evangelist ministers, yet he did.

Another strident voice professing the Ford brand of Americanism was the self-proclaimed superpatriot Elizabeth Elios Dilling. Wife of a minor Chicago politician, this woman launched an attack on everyone she suspected of being a Communist sympathizer, which, in her case, was just about everyone left of George Washington. In her first book, *The Red Network: A Handbook of Radicalism for Patriots*, she listed 460 "Communist, Anarchist, Socialist . . . controlled organizations and 1,300 individuals who have contributed in some measure to one or more phases of the Red movement in the United States." The organizations she deemed dangerous included the Methodist Federation, the American Federation of Labor, the National Association for the Advancement of Colored People, the American Federation of Teachers, the YMCA, and the YWCA. And her subversives list reads like a who's who in liberal and intellectual America. Jane Addams, Eleanor Roosevelt, Justice Brandeis, and most members of Congress made her list. Dilling's reasons for branding individuals "Red" were absurd, but many took the accusations seriously in the frightened thirties. Of Einstein she wrote, "While I am unable to understand the scientific value of the Relativity Theory, I can understand the 'relativity' of Einstein to his daughter, who married a Russian. . . . Another of Einstein's qualifications as a dangerous enemy to our institutions is the fact that he has been President Roosevelt's overnight White House guest."

In her two major books and numerous pamphlets, Dilling expressed both anti-Semitic and pro-Fascist ideas. "Most of the Communists are Jews," she concluded. "The savage Mohammedan call of the muezzin as heard in darkest Asia is mingled with the propaganda of the Hindu, Jew and Agnostic. . . . God created separate races but Communists insist on racial intermixture and intermarriage. Neither the races nor the sexes can ever be equal." As for Fascism, she was more than benevolent: "It seeks a harmony between all classes and concedes to industrialists, white-collar, professional as well as laboring workers, a place in the social order as necessary parts, not as 'class enemies,' of the whole, but under state control. It defends some property rights and religion. . . . The problem of the large number of revolutionary Russian Jews in Germany doubtless contributed toward making Fascist Germany anti-Semitic. . . . It [Fascism] is the only enemy feared by the Reds, because it is the only system which opposes militancy and puts down the dictatorship with another. . . . As the strength of Socialism-Communism increases, the chance to preserve Democracy decreases, until eventually fascism becomes the only alternative to Socialism-Communism."[18]

Despite the idiocy of her writings, they became standard literature for anti-Semitic and Nazi organizations up to World War II. Winrod, in fact, gave a free copy of Dilling's *Red Network* to anyone subscribing to the *The Revealer*. She had no public connection with Henry Ford, but Harry Bennett, Ford's service department chief, quite out of character for him, became a significant financial contributor to Elizabeth Dilling's writings and speaking engagements.[19] He is known to have given $5,000 on one occasion.[20]

While most of these American groups were "only" pro-Fascist, at least one took its orders directly from the Nazi party. The organization bore several names from the late twenties up to America's entry into World War II, when it was quashed. At first it was called the Teutonia Clubs, then the Friends of Germany, then the Friends of New Germany, and finally the German-American Bund. The founders of the Teutonia Clubs admitted before congressional investigators that they had taken orders directly from headquarters in Germany. That was apparent in 1933, when Rudolf Hess, head of the political section of the National Socialist party, showed concern about rising anti-Nazi sentiment in the United States by ordering the American organization to disband, only to reform days later as the Friends of New Germany. The guise was an attempt to make the American Nazi organization look native-born. Yet they retained in the oath of membership the statement: "I am of Aryan descent, free of Jewish or colored racial traces."[21]

The American Nazis found a friendly home in Ford's factory system. Sander Diamond in *The Nazi Movement in the U.S.* confirms that "many members of the Teutonia Association were

94

employed by Ford Motor Company." It was later revealed that Heinz Spanknoebel, the American Nazi party's first Führer, "got his original propaganda money by working for Ford."[22] Spanknoebel returned to Germany after conviction for serving a foreign government without registering. Detective Casimir Palmer, who had been involved as a government intelligence agent since Boris Brasol brought the *Protocols* to America, wrote to Professor Nathan Isaacs in 1937 that "Henry Ford and his subordinates Ernest G. Liebold, W. J. Cameron, Harry Bennett, and others have turned the Ford Motor Company Chemical Department into the headquarters of the Nazis here."[23] In 1940 a publication favoring the Allies would write, "It may be significant that every time Hitler's efforts bogged down in New York, Chicago, or other cities of substantial German-American population, men from Detroit, amply supplied with funds, revived them."[24]

One Ford employee, an American Nazi, was especially visible. He was Fritz Kuhn, an American citizen of German birth who had been with Hitler briefly in the early years of the Führer's political development. Kuhn came to power when, once again, the organization underwent a name change, from Friends to Bund. The German-American Bund was to appear to be led by Americans, thus leaving it less subject to suspicion as a foreign propaganda tool. Yet, of course, the guise was thin. Federal investigations concluded that the Bund definitely "came into existence with explicit instructions from Germany to carry on propaganda without antagonizing the whole country." Kuhn at first seemed like the right man for the job. He rose quickly from Detroit local chief to Midwestern chief and finally to the national leadership, all based on his dynamic speech-making ability and his willingness to follow orders from Berlin. Kuhn had a fatal flaw, however, in that he was a thief. In Germany in

1921 he was caught ransacking the pockets of fellow students at the university. In an odd quirk of fate, he was saved from prison by a family friend—a Jewish businessman named Reinhold Spitz. Kuhn was given a job in Spitz's warehouse, where he was promptly caught stealing. Instead of notifying the police, Spitz gave Kuhn money to go to Mexico for a new start. Soon, Kuhn was in Detroit applying for American citizenship, and spreading anti-Semitic propaganda.

Under Kuhn the Bund took on all of the trappings of the Hitler movement in Germany. Members wore armbands with swastikas, German storm trooper-like uniforms, and, with arms raised in the Nazi salute, recited the motto: "To a free, gentile-ruled United States and to our fighting movement of awakened Aryan Americans, a threefold, rousing 'Free America. Free America. Free America.'" The various locals were organized as in Germany, complete with youth groups which were carbon copies of the Hitler Youth Movement. Kuhn even took a delegation of Bund members to Berlin during the 1936 Olympics, where he met briefly with Hitler. It was also revealed later that he and other Bund members performed intelligence work for the Nazi regime. Unfortunately for Kuhn, his old habit of placing fingers in pockets caught up with him in 1939. He was tried and convicted of grand larceny in the embezzlement of Bund funds. He was sent to Sing Sing Prison where he sat out World War II. Even after his conviction, Bund newspapers defended him. Kuhn was the first German-American prisoner of war, they said, a victim of anti-German persecution.[25]

Kuhn's career at Ford was sporadic. He worked from August 1928 through December 12, 1929, in the Ford Hospital chemistry department. He then was absent from the payrolls for six months while doing party work, returning to a job at the Rouge heat-treat operation in June 1930, where he stayed for only three months before leaving again. Then he was rehired in February 1931 and held his Ford job for the next five and a half years until his duties in the Bund forced him to quit in July 1936.[26]

Rudolph Heupel, a Bund committee member and close friend of Kuhn's, said Kuhn was not popular with fellow Rouge workers because of his vocal expressions of Nazism. "But he was popular with Ford officials because of his Nazi leanings because ... they know that Herr Ford is a militant Jew-hater." Under pressure, Heupel later denied making the statement about Kuhn at Ford.[27] But Kuhn himself did speak of his affiliation. In 1937, returning from his audience with Hitler, Kuhn told reporters, "I was really on vacation when I left the [Ford] company's employ and I don't know when or whether I will return to my old job. I am a marked man now, and Mr. Ford might not want me."[28] The final contact came in December 1939. A *Detroit News* reporter saw Henry Ford in the crowd at Grand Central Station. Kuhn was sitting in a rail car under guard on his way to serve his prison sentence. According to the report, Ford looked into the train at Kuhn, made no comment, and left.[29]

To understand how such activities could have gone on within the Ford plant system, one must first realize how that environment had changed since the inception of the five-dollar day had made Ford workers the envy of American labor. As the competitors at Chevrolet and Chrysler began to gain ground on Ford, his solution was invariably to cut the price of his cars—down to $260 for a Model T Run-about at one point. To do this meant constant speedups of the asembly line and elimination of as many workers as possible. Ford Motor Company became known as the worst sweatshop in Detroit. Its workers lived in constant fear of firing if they didn't keep the pace. Workers were thrown out for talking, smoking, or even frowning on the job. Meal breaks were fifteen minutes, and workers were expected to run to the rest rooms. By the mid-thirties, the high pay once granted the Ford worker had dwindled to the lowest wages in the industry. Beneficent paternalism was gone. The attitude from the top down was a hard line toward the employees. Samuel Marquis, a former employee and friend of Henry Ford's, said he was told by a Ford executive who subscribed to the new philosophy that "one must maintain an attitude toward the employees that makes them fear and hate you. I am the most fortunate man in the organization, because everyone despises me."[30]

From his public retraction in 1927 on, observers noticed that Ford's actions increasingly reflected a preoccupation with violence. And nowhere is this preoccupation better personified than in the meteoric rise to power in the company of Harry Bennett. Ford hired Bennett in 1916 when journalist Arthur Brisbane had seen the young man brawling in the streets and took him to meet Mr. Ford. Bennett was a small man, just five foot seven and 145 pounds, yet he was afraid of nothing. He had been a prizefighter in the navy and would challenge anyone at the slightest opportunity. Ford brought him in and kept him around the plants as a titleless errand boy. Henry liked to start fights, Bennett said in his biography. "Harry, let's you and him have a fight," he'd say, but before they could go to it, Ford would always leave the room.[31]

Bennett gained power through sheer force. He created a small army of thugs—boxers, underworld figures, and ex-convicts. He positioned his men as bosses and, more often, as spies. If anyone in the plants was caught doing anything deemed foolish, such as talking to a union organizer, he would be beaten up and fired. The American Civil Liberties Union wrote to Ford in 1932,

"Harry Bennett seems clearly committed to a policy of violence, espionage, and lawlessness. It has been charged on reliable authority that your police force is connected with gangsters and racketeers of the underworld."[32] Bennett's service department soon became a veritable secret police organization. It was estimated that between the foremen, the service department men, and the spies, there were fifteen overseers for every 100 employees.[33]

Ralph Rimar, who worked in the service department under Bennett, said, "Our gestapo covered Dearborn with a thick web of corruption, intimidation, and intrigue. The spy net was all-embracing. My own agents reported back to me conversations in grocery stores, meat markets, and restaurants, gambling joints, beer gardens, social groups, boys' clubs, and even churches. Women waiting in markets buying something might discuss their husbands' jobs and activities; if they did, I soon heard what they said. To those who have never lived under dictatorship it is difficult to convey the sense of fear which is part of the Ford system."[34]

Bennett's power did not end at the factory gate. He reached out to form ties with Mafia men through use of his patronage powers. Chester Lamare, a Sicilian with seventeen arrests in Detroit, for example, was given the fresh fruit concession at the Rouge. "Chet didn't know a banana from an orange," Bennett boasted. He also made contact with the East Coast Mafia by giving the car-hauling business to Tony D'Anna.

As Henry Ford became more obsessed that Jewish bankers and Communists were attempting to infiltrate his company and take over, Bennett's power grew. He fed on Ford's fears by starting rumors, stories of elaborate plots and tales of threats to kidnap Ford's grandsons which indirectly reached the old man. Bennett's success at intimidating the witness in the Sapiro case, and acting as intermediary for the public retraction, bought him Ford's favor. His value to Ford, which even Bennett admitted, was that he would do whatever his master bid without question. Soon, Bennett had more power in the company than Liebold or even Ford's son Edsel.

Bennett firmly maintained that he was neither anti-Semitic nor pro-Fascist, a statement which was probably true, yet he ran his operation as if he were both, obviously attempting to please a higher authority. Once, for instance, Henry Ford was telling an employee that a group of Jews had been behind the assassination of Abraham Lincoln. When Ford was asked if he could document the facts, he said, "Oh, no doubt about the facts. Harry Bennett has made an investigation."[35]

Philip Slomovitz, editor of Detroit's *Jewish News*, went to lunch with Bennett and asked about his anti-Semitism. "He kept saying he wasn't anti-Semitic," Slomovitz said, "but everything he'd say refuted his own words."[36] In 1936, union men charged that foremen were distributing anti-Semitic literature throughout the plants. The material blamed the world's ills on the Jews and repeatedly referred to President Roosevelt as "Rosenfelt."[37] According to the complaint, "The Ford service men, who are plentiful in this as in other departments, were fully aware of this distribution of anti-Semitic and anti-Catholic propaganda, for much of it was done directly under their eyes." By 1939, the anti-Semitic atmosphere at the Rouge plants had gotten much stronger. Signs appeared on the gates of the employee parking lots which read: "Jews are traitors to America and should not be trusted—Buy Gentile." Another sign proclaimed:

Jews Teach Communism
Jews Teach Atheism

100

Jews Destroy Christianity
Jews Control the Press
Jews Produce Filthy Movies
Jews Control Money[38]

Pro-fascism and anti-Semitism seemed to go together at Ford. Ralph Rimar, the Bennett lieutenant, said: "Pro-Fascist ideas flourished in the Ford labor spy ring. . . . I found and heard repeated among my colleagues instances of actual Fascist sympathies. . . . I established data establishing the Nazi connections of about fifteen men, several of them in important jobs. . . . But each time I inquired afterward, I got no result." The report was "upstairs," he was told, which was reason enough to drop the subject. Rimar also says that the Ford service men themselves spread anti-Semitic ideas. "We told the Negroes the Jews were leading the union," he said. "We tried to divide the men, not only white against black, but also Jew against Gentile."[39]

While fascism and anti-Semitism were games played to please the boss, Bennett's ultimate task throughout the 1930s was to keep the Congress of Industrial Organizations (C.I.O.) out of the Ford plants. Henry Ford had said he would never recognize the United Automobile Workers of America (U.A.W.). When the workers struck for union recognition in the mid-thirties, Ford said, "The international financiers are really back of these strikes. . . . The whole object of the strikes is to kill competition, and we are about the only competition that financiers have at this time. They'll not get anywhere while I'm alive."[40]

Bennett's task was to stop them, but Ford no longer was willing to take on his opponents directly, to risk courts, more controversy, and lost sales. So Bennett sought outside allies and, in so doing, inspired or encouraged far greater anti-Semitic activity than ever before. Radicals like Winrod, Dilling, Edmonson, and, more discretely, Cameron, could connect the idea of unionism and Jewish Communism in the popular mind. But their influence was limited. Bennett needed and sought out far more powerful and credible figures.

Bennett's main ally against the unionists turned out to be an unlikely choice at first glance. Father Charles Coughlin was a Roman Catholic priest and staunch supporter of Roosevelt's New Deal in the early 1930s. Henry Ford disliked Catholics and was bitterly opposed to Roosevelt's administration. Yet in 1936, about the time connections between Ford's men and Coughlin began to surface, the priest had a change of heart. He renounced Roosevelt and the New Deal and began espousing the Populist and anti-Semitic line characteristic of Ford in the days of the *Dearborn Independent.*

Coughlin was known as the "Radio Priest." He began radio sermons at station WJR in Detroit in 1926 to raise money for his parish, the Shrine of the Little Flower, in Royal Oak, Michigan. For four years he gave children's talks, then gradually moved into politics and economics. He was an excellent speaker, with the fine-spun brogue of the Irish upper class and a way of turning a phrase that was both amusing and meaningful. In 1932, when the Columbia Broadcasting Company and National Broadcasting Company both turned down his program, Coughlin created his own network, which expanded to forty-seven stations from Maine to Colorado. At his peak of popularity, Coughlin's listeners numbered between 30 and 40 million. His publication, *Social Justice,* began in 1936 and soon achieved more than 1 million circulation.

Coughlin's theme was that capitalism was doomed and really not worth saving. Instead, he proposed a system of fascist controls under the broad heading of "social justice." He came out firmly for elimination of the gold standard and for isolationism, control of labor, and outlawing of strikes. Communist Jews were behind all of America's problems, he concluded in 1936. All of this brought him completely in line with Ford's thinking.

Coughlin introduced a new level of deception into the old lies by using different techniques. His favorite ploy was to cite an obscure publication as the authority for a historical revelation. For example, Coughlin asserted that the American Civil War was fought for freedom from the Jewish bankers. He credited a book titled *The Rothschilds* by John Reeves, which had been out of print since 1887. Coughlin liked to recite this quote, attributed by Reeves to Disraeli at a Rothschild family gathering: "Under this roof are the heads of the family of Rothschild—a name famous in every capital of Europe and every division of the globe. *If you like, we shall divide the United States into two parts, one for you, James, and one for you, Lionel. Napoleon [III] will do exactly [what] and all that I shall advise him.*"

An enterprising reporter on the *Chicago Daily News* dug out a copy of the original book and found Coughlin had modified the quote, which actually read: "Under this roof are the heads of the family of Rothschild—a name famous in every capital of Europe and every division of the globe—*a family not more regarded for its riches than esteemed for its honor, virtues, and public spirit.*"

Coughlin often professed to have highly confidential material in his possession which proved a point he wished to make. Occasionally he would even give names. He stated that two Polish rabbis, Rudolph Fleischman and a Rabbi Grunfeld, had verified that the *Protocols* were authentic. A leader of the Polish rabbinate responded that no such men ever existed in his country. On another occasion, Coughlin claimed information from the U.S. Secret Service that proved Jews financed the Russian revolution. The head of the Secret Service said that the report Coughlin referred to never existed. To all of these rebuttals, Coughlin would choose not to respond. "The only real authority for the truth," he once said, "is Father Coughlin."[41]

While Father Coughlin denounced the C.I.O. as a Communist organization, the National Labor Relations Board began receiving affidavits that Henry Ford was financing the Radio Priest. Rimer, while still in the Ford service department, said that "the company was collaborating with Father Coughlin in the era of his best violent antidemocratic, anti-Semitic oratory. In return for Coughlin's sympathy, the company bought large quantities of *Social Justice* magazine."

A common technique for fighting unions has been to introduce a new, puppet union to split the workers' loyalties and prevent a major union from becoming established. Father Coughlin attempted to establish such a union at Ford. He organized the "Workers Council for Social Justice," a labor union from which Jews were excluded. "The new Christian Union has no quarrel with the Brahman, the Buddhist, or the Jew. The Workers Council for Social Justice . . . will not compromise nor accept the principles of these philosophies, which are in conflict with Christianity," he stated. Ford Motor Company, Coughlin maintained, could be encouraged to use its assets for the benefit of employees. One manifestation would be company stores selling foods and clothing at cost to employees. The Workers Council, however, did not work. Ford workers were simply not interested, and within weeks of its announcement, the idea was abandoned.

Coughlin also acted as a go-between for Bennett. He invited Homer Martin, President of the U.A.W., to his church quarters for dinner. Coughlin suggested to Martin that he should "strike out on his own," establishing his own labor union. In that way, Martin "could do more for the workingman than by taking orders from John L. Lewis and his Red henchmen." Coughlin suggested unionizing Ford with the new organization, and set up a meeting with Harry Bennett to discuss it. Martin soon began accepting large sums of money from Bennett just to "support good unionism." On several occasions, Coughlin entered the scene again, offering to give Martin a building for a union headquarters. The building he offered was worth as much as $150,000. Finally, Bennett announced that he would allow a new union to organize Ford workers and that Homer Martin would be the chief union executive. This scheme, however, failed as miserably as Coughlin's Workers Councils.[42]

Failing to become a union boss, Coughlin reached out in a new direction. He announced a new organization called the Christian Front. Members would be organized into small groups, or platoons as he called them. Within weeks, thousands of these platoons sprang up among his radio followers. The organization was remarkably aggressive, following what Coughlin called the Franco way to "meet force with force as a last result." According to the literature, the Christian Front did not fear the label of fascist, since it was only a part of the Communists' attack strategy. The organization would be "a Christian Front which will not fear to be called 'anti-Semitic' because it knows the term 'anti-Semitic' is only another pet phrase of castigation in Communism's glossary of attack."

This appeal to racism and violence took a nasty turn. Christian Front groups accumulated weapons and fought openly at rallies. More than 233 arrests were made during this period. In New York, Christian Front leader John Cassidy organized what he called sports clubs, which were essentially vigilante groups which would take to the streets "to protect their rights by force." The F.B.I. soon arrested thirteen members and confiscated their weapons, which included bombs, rifles, and dynamite stolen from National Guard armories. J. Edgar Hoover said the group planned to kill Jews, Communists, and a dozen congressmen who were thought to be sympathizers, and to seize several federal buildings. This was to be accomplished by a cooperative move by Christian Fronters and German-American Bund members.

Although Coughlin professed his anti-Semitism in 1936, he did not begin publishing anti-Semitic material until 1938. But when he began, he opened up with a full-scale barrage. He started by publishing the *Protocols of the Learned Elders of Zion* in *Social Justice*. "Yes, the Jews have always claimed that the *Protocols* were forgeries," Coughlin wrote in the introduction, "but I prefer the words of Henry Ford, who said, 'The best test of the truth of the *Protocols* is in the fact that up to the present minute they have been carried out.'" In a letter defending his position, Coughlin said, "Mr. Ford did retract his accusations against the Jews. But neither Mr. Ford nor I retract the statement that many of the events predicted in the *Protocols* have come to pass."[43]

Just as Coughlin was opening up with the *Protocols,* a familiar face appeared at the *Social Justice* magazine offices. Boris Brasols, the tsarist who brought the *Protocols* to Ford, now appeared to be writing for Coughlin. Detective Casimir Palmer recognized Brasol when he saw him entering the home of one of Coughlin's top aides, and reported that Brasol was writing for Coughlin under the name of Ben Marcin. The *Protocols* and a number of articles accusing the Jewish banking house of Kuhn, Loeb, and Company of financing the Bolshevik revolution had appeared under the Ben Marcin byline. Palmer said that while Brasol was paid in cash, eliminating evidence, he had confirmation of Brasol's involvement at *Social Justice* through a financial broker of the magazine. Brasol was also identified with the German-American Bund at the same time. He had made repeated trips to Germany and was lavish in his praise of Adolf Hitler.[44]

Brasol's presence and the Ford influence may help to explain Father Coughlin's ever-increasing leanings toward Fascism. Coughlin named Mussolini *Social Justice*'s "Man of the Week." He defended the Italian dictator's persecution of Jews on the grounds that "most Jews were anti-Fascist." He did not criticize Hitler for taking Austria, and parroted the Nazi rationale for their invasion of the Sudetenland, claiming that the ethnic Germans in the area had been mistreated. "Nazism," Coughlin said, "was conceived as a defense against Communism." He once ran a photograph of Hitler in *Social Justice* and a story admitting Hitler had persecuted Catholics, Protestants, and Jews, but apologized for him, suggesting that, after all, no one is perfect. He claimed that Hitler's anti-Semitism was at least partly engendered by a speech delivered by Samuel Untermeyer in 1933, a talk which defended German Jews and offended the Führer.[45]

Coughlin's condolences for the mistreatment of Jews in Germany were expressed in such a way that he actually was saying that the Jews brought the hardships on themselves. The Jews deserved no pity because "they have shown no sympathy for the persecuted in other lands." The ultimate proof of his Nazi affiliation surfaced when Coughlin published an article under his own byline which presented an emotional argument that the Jews were behind the Communist takeover in Russia. Coughlin titled it "Background for Persecution." The article was actually

107

a speech given by Nazi propaganda minister Joseph Goebbels at the Seventh National Socialist Congress on September 13, 1935. Two examples from the texts should prove the point. First, Coughlin:

> The atheist Jew, Gubermann, under the name of Jaroslawski and then the leader of the militant atheists in Soviet Union, also declared: "It is our duty to destroy every religious world concept. If the destruction of 10 million human beings, as happened in the last war, should be necessary for the triumph of one definite class, then that must be done, and it will be done."

Now Goebbels:

> The Jew, Gubermann, who, under the name of Jaroslawski, is the leader of the Association of Militant Atheists in the Soviet Union, has made the following declaration: "It is our duty to destroy every religious world concept. . . . If the destruction of 10 million human beings, as happened in the last war, should be necessary for the triumph of one definite class, then that must be done, and it will be done."

Again Coughlin:

> In 1919 Hungary, a neighbor to Germany, was overrun with Communists. The notorious atheist, Bela Kun, a Jew whose real name was Aaron Cohn, murdered 20,000.

And Goebbels:

> In 1919, during the Bolshevik regime of Bela Kun, a Jew, whose

108

real name was Aaron Cohn, in Budapest was involved when twenty hostages were murdered.

Except for the exaggeration of the number murdered—Coughlin found it hard to resist bolstering figures—the two texts are virtually identical. Coughlin did not even bother to modify phrases or shift paragraphs around. He was willing to lend Goebbels' words his own audience and the credibility of a man of the cloth.

Julius Streicher's notorious Jew-baiting magazine, *Der Stür-mer,* praised Coughlin for "flaying the Jews." And *Look* magazine revealed a relationship between Coughlin and Bund leader Fritz Kuhn. "Father Coughlin and Kuhn are good friends," the article reported. "Kuhn tried to get him to take off his collar and go into politics, but Father Coughlin wouldn't do it. He can't do much because of his collar."[46] Soon after, at a "Mass Demonstration for True Americanism" attended by 20,000 pro-Fascists in New York City, the crowd rendered ear-splitting applause when the names Hitler, Mussolini, Franco, and Father Coughlin were raised in the context of the speeches.[47]

Attempts were made to counter Coughlin's fantastic claims. The Anti-Defamation League, the American Jewish Committee, the American Jewish Congress, and the Jewish Labor Committee joined forces in a new organization, the General Jewish Council. Attempting to expose the real facts, the council published a monograph entitled *Father Coughlin: His "Facts" and Arguments.* Former New York Governor Alfred E. Smith, the leading lay Catholic of his day, introduced the work as follows: "When a man presumes to address so great a number of listeners as Father Coughlin reaches, particularly if he is a priest, he assumes the responsibility of not misleading them by false statements or poisoning their judgments with baseless slanders. From boyhood I was taught that a Catholic priest was under the divine injunction to 'teach the nations' the word of God. That includes the divine commandment 'Thou shalt not bear false witness against thy neighbor.' "[48]

Still another ecclesiastic professing the doctrine shared by Ford in the late 1930s was Reverend Gerald L. K. Smith, a former member of the fascist Silver Shirts. Like Coughlin, Smith drew his following with radio sermons and his publication, *The Cross and the Flag.* Unlike Coughlin, Smith was a rabid anti-Semite with so little sophistication that he was never able to gain a mass following. At times, however, he could draw upward of 20,000 supporters to a rally. Smith's thesis differed hardly a whit from Ford's. International Jewish bankers were the world's problem, the C.I.O. and all labor organizations were Communist, and the New Deal was "the Jew Deal." He added the Cameron argument that "the Jews are largely not descended from the Israelites of the Bible, but sprang from a tribe of roving bandits."[49]

Ford's support of Smith was more open. At a Smith anti-Communist rally, Ford provided him with a full complement of bodyguards from his service department.[50] Ford, of course, did not contribute directly to Smith's campaigns; Bennett did. The extent of the contributions is not known, but there is documentation that Bennett paid for at least three of Smith's radio broadcasts on station WJR in Detroit.[51] Smith did Bennett's bidding in return. At one time he put on a series of revivalist rallies in Dearborn to support one of Bennett's candidates in a fiercely contested local election. Smith, however, abused his friendship with Ford by speaking too frequently of it and quoting the old man freely. Ford once said, "I wish Gerald L. K. Smith could be president of the United States," a comment Smith publicized

110

ever after. Ford confided to Smith that "I hope to republish the *International Jew* again sometime," and Smith spoke openly of that, as well. Eventually Ford broke with Smith, refusing to fund him in any way. Yet Smith never ceased admiring Ford or drawing on the *Dearborn Independent* propaganda and Ford's version of the *Protocols* as the inspiration for his crusade against the Jews.[52]

Here, then, is the apologetic Henry Ford. He no longer frothed at reporters about the Jewish menace. He still blamed all evil on the international financiers, but now he was careful not to link the word *Jew* to them. Looking at his public statements between 1927 and 1938, it is easy to assume that Ford had in fact rejected his Jew phobia. The truth is that he no longer needed to expose himself to ridicule nor run the risk of boycotts against his products, for others would carry on his vendetta. William Cameron, Harry Bennett, Gerald Winrod, Elizabeth Dilling, Father Charles Coughlin, the Reverend Gerald L. K. Smith, and the entire German-American Bund movement would mouth his sentiments. Some of these people were truly Ford puppets; others merely cooperated with him and relied upon their own convictions for motivation. For some, like Bennett, there was power to be gained; for others, like Winrod and perhaps Coughlin, there was access to great wealth. Smith felt genuine adulation for Ford; and a very few others, like Cameron, may well have entertained a sincere belief in the ideology of racism. These were the people with whom Henry Ford allied his power. How stark the contrast with what Wendell Willkie said when he rejected Father Coughlin's support for president against Roosevelt: "I am not interested in his support," Willkie said. "I don't have to be president of the United States, but I do have to live with myself."[53]

6

Ford's Final Thrust

•

Henry Ford's deceptive silence was shattered in July of 1933 by his distant admirer, Adolf Hitler. On the occasion of Ford's seventy-fifth birthday, Hitler sent personal congratulations, along with the highest honor which could be awarded by the Nazi government: the Grand Cross of the German Eagle. Ford shared this honor with only four other men, one of them Mussolini. As if to flag the underlying reasons for this great honor, Ernest Liebold, former president of the *Dearborn Independent*, received the second highest honor of the Reich government, the First Order of the German Eagle, two weeks later.[1] The awards served as a spotlight, drawing attention to Ford's pro-fascist and anti-Semitic past, and prompting journalists and investigators to look closer at the Ford operation. It also either inspired or coincided with Henry Ford's return to center stage, where he would again make his anti-Semitism known.

113

Ford had been urged by many not to accept the award. Another industrialist, Thomas J. Watson of International Business Machines Corporation, had been given a lesser medal that same year but returned it to protest Hitler's militarism. Ford could have done the same, but instead he not only accepted the award, he accepted it in a public ceremony in which German Consul Fritz Hailer draped the medal across Ford's chest before enthusiastic onlookers, who included Cameron and Liebold. Ford's only response to the public upon receiving the decoration was that he accepted it not from the German government but from the people of Germany. Privately he said, "They sent me this ribbon band. They [the Americans] told me to return it or else I'm not an American. I'm going to keep it." Liebold was far more effusive in his thanks to the Führer. In a letter expressing his deep-felt appreciation, Liebold wrote, "An occasion of this kind becomes one of the outstanding events in our life's history, and leaves an everlasting impression on our memory."[2]

The impression the award made on American Jewry was real and immediate. Jewish leaders denounced Ford's acceptance. The National Encampment Committee of the Jewish War Veterans of the United States said the award indicated Ford's "endorsement of the German-American Bund and their subversive un-American activities and other anti-democratic groups." Entertainer Eddie Cantor expressed the general feeling best when he said that Ford "is a damn fool for permitting the world's greatest gangster to give him a citation." Sales of Ford and Lincoln cars dropped to a new low in New York and other cities with large Jewish populations.[3]

The product boycott, not organized, but effective, frightened the marketing men within Ford Motor Company into urging Ford to make some kind of public statement which would placate the Jews, as he had in 1927. Again, they decided that a prominent Jewish spokesman could carry the message most effectively, and that Dr. Leo Franklin, Ford's former neighbor and friend, would be the right one for the task. Since there had been no contact between Franklin and Ford for years, and all of Franklin's letters protesting the continued distribution of the *International Jew* had been ignored, it was clear they would have to convince the distinguished rabbi to meet with Ford. To do this, they approached Moritz Kahn, brother of architect Albert Kahn, and one of the few Jews who had not broken with Ford over the years. The carrot was that Ford had expressed sincere concern over the problem of Jewish refugees from Germany, an effort in which Dr. Franklin was personally involved. Ford, they said, would like to talk about hiring more of these people, but first Franklin should write a letter to Ford formally requesting the meeting. The necessity for a letter should have been a tip-off to Franklin that something was wrong with the proposal, but since he had always believed that Ford was fundamentally a good man who was simply misinformed about the Jews, Franklin took the bait and sent the letter. Two more intermediaries, Harry Bennett and Harry Newman, a former All-American football player and a Jew, finally arranged the actual meeting in Bennett's office at the Ford Administration Building in Dearborn.

The meeting was warm and open. Franklin spoke for over an hour with Ford, Bennett, Cameron, and Newman. Ford emphasized his concern over the German Jewish refugee problem and said he fully intended to hire as many of these displaced people as he could. Franklin was asked to help draft a letter to the public announcing this decision. Cameron and Franklin worked out the wording, then Ford endorsed the letter and even posed for a picture with Franklin. The letter itself was firm and direct. It condemned the persecution in Germany, stating the belief that it was not the will of the people but of a few Nazi leaders. America is the "haven for the oppressed," it said, and Ford for his part would do everything possible to give the displaced Jew "an opportunity to rebuild his life."

Franklin was next asked to deliver the letter to the newspapers in person. After leaving, however, he had some second thoughts about the wording and, making a few changes, called Bennett back for confirmation. Ford again approved the letter's contents, and Franklin then delivered it to the two leading Detroit newspapers. Before the statement appeared in print, Franklin received an anonymous call from someone who identified himself only as a former Ford service department agent. The caller said that Franklin was being used and would be double-crossed by Ford, Bennett, and Father Coughlin. Dr. Franklin ignored the call.

The following evening, Father Coughlin began a vehement attack on the international Jewish bankers and other devious Jews, such as Rabbi Leo Franklin, whom Coughlin maintained was the real author of the recent Ford statement. The letter, Coughlin said, was totally inaccurate. It represented "not what Ford had actually said, but what Franklin wished he would have said." The priest said that "Mr. Harry Bennett, Ford personnel manager, speaking officially for the Ford Motor Company, permits us to use the following in a signed statement:

"1. The direct quotation carried in the paper [The *Detroit News*] is totally inaccurate and was not written by Mr. Ford but was composed by Rabbi Franklin.

"2. Rabbi Franklin came to see Mr. Ford to ask him if his factory would assimilate Jewish refugees, the result of Nazi

116

persecution. Mr. Ford said that he believed there was little or no persecution in Germany; if any, it was due not to the German government, but to the warmongers, the international bankers."[4]

After Coughlin's radio attack and a follow-up article in *Social Justice,* newsmen asked Bennett to comment on the Coughlin story. Bennett corroborated Coughlin's story, except for the statement that it was "totally" inaccurate. Franklin, Bennett said, came to him first to arrange the meeting (proof was the letter Franklin sent requesting the audience with Ford). "Mr. Ford did not attack the German government and did not mention Nazism, and any persecution, if there was any, was not the fault of Hitler or the Nazis." Bennett, however, did not seem completely satisfied with Father Coughlin's performance and was heard to say, "He crossed me up. I am going to get in touch with him and tell him so."[5]

The *Detroit Free Press* came out in strong support of Dr. Franklin's story. His reputation in the community was such, they said, that no one should question it. Coughlin, the paper wrote, had a "congenital inability to tell the truth." The priest sued the newspaper for $4 million, but backed down when the *Free Press* produced a massive volume of contradictory statements Coughlin had made. Bennett also eventually backed down, admitting that the letter was accurate and expressed Ford's sentiments. These final statements, coming well after the incident, received little publicity.

The statement and confused denial were far more meaningful than a simple vicious trick on a gentle old rabbi. They were a poorly designed attempt to project two opposite images of Ford for different constituencies. To the Jewish community seeing the letter and firm support for the German Jew's plight, Henry Ford becomes a kind and supportive soul. They might even be moved to buy his cars. The anti-Semitic Americans and Hitlerites could point to the denial to show that Ford was still with them in spirit, and that once again the Flivver King had been deceived by a Jew. The fact that Ford was willing to deeply hurt a trusting old friend was presumably irrelevant.

Such ploys threw few intelligent people off Ford's scent. Hitler's medal was too absolute a tribute to ignore, especially by the anti-Fascist forces that were coalescing as Hitler began to consume Europe in the late 1930s. If the award were not enough, there were other strong indictments of Ford's position. In any of some 800 Nazi publications in circulation, Ford was being eulogized, and his name appeared in the Nazi book list as author of *The Jewish Question,* the German-American Bund's new title for the *International Jew.*[6] The Ku Klux Klan was also publishing the *International Jew,* with credit to Ford, in its publication *The Fiery Cross.* And Cameron continued to sell the *International Jew* through the Anglo-Saxon Federation. The anti-Fascists were righteously determined to make Ford a target in their publications such as *PM* and *Friday,* and once they began to dig, there was abundant ammunition to be found.

High-ranking employees in Ford's worldwide operation were often exposed as pro-Nazi. Gaston Bergery, Ford's business representative in Paris, was named by the Sunday *New York Times* as "the coming man" in the Nazi movement in that country. Ford of Mexico manager Julio Brunet was found to be giving support to the Mexican Fascist Gold Shirt leader General Nicholas Rodriguez. The head of Ford of Britain, Lord Perry, was considered "intimate" with members of the pro-Nazi circle. And the head of Ford of Germany, Edmund Heine, was suspected of selling military plans to the Hitler government. Later,

Heine would be tried and convicted of espionage when he returned to the United States. A Detroit attorney with close working ties to Ford's staff drew attention when he sent a telegram of congratulations to Hitler when he seized Czechoslovakia. In 1939, a General George Van Horn Moseley was brought before a Senate investigation committee because of a plot by Nazi leaders to overthrow the U.S. government and install Moseley as ruler. Cameron rushed to his defense in the pages of *Destiny*.[7]

Even Edsel Ford was unable to avoid suspicion, since he was found to be a director and part owner of the General Aniline Corporation, with partners including Carl Bosch, a Hitler backer since 1926, and Wilhelm von Rath of Germany. In 1941, federal agents would raid the company's New York offices. The vice-president of the company, Rudolph Hutz, was interned as a spy on charges that he was delivering documents, code books, maps, blueprints of military planes, and other information to the German government.[8]

Ford didn't allay the suspicions when he refused to build aircraft engines for England while building five-ton military trucks for Germany.[9] Ford's minions worked out a barter deal with the Nazi regime whereby Ford would ship rubber and metals to Germany and give the Nazi government 30 percent of the cargo, all this despite clear evidence of Germany's growing bellicosity between 1937 and 1939. In 1939, Ford Motor Company concluded a deal to build command cars and troop carriers, with a design supplied by the German high command. The German Ford Werke's employee publication irritated anti-Fascists by praising Hitler and boasting of their contribution to Nazi military production. One line in the publication read: "At the beginning of this year we vowed to give our best and utmost

119

for final victory, in unshakable faithfulness to our Führer. Today we say with pride that we succeeded." In the spring of 1939, Ford and Germany remembered the Führer's birthday, and on Hitler's fiftieth the company sent him a gift of 50,000 reichsmarks.[10] Ford Motor Company also created a public furor when, just six months after the Japanese attacked China, the manager of Ford of Japan announced the purchase of $290,000 worth of Japanese war bonds.[11]

Ford's image was not helped when, in 1940, he became the godfather of Prince Louis Ferdinand's second son. Ferdinand was the oldest surviving grandson of the former German kaiser; the emperor himself showed sympathy for Adolf Hitler in the early 1930s. Ford all but adopted Ferdinand, employing him for a while with the nebulous title of "free-lance roadman." Ferdinand traveled extensively for Ford, including trips to Nazi Germany. Although he broke with Hitler eventually and even became a friend of President Roosevelt, Ferdinand was widely viewed as an anti-Semite. And corroboration is to be found in correspondence from Ferdinand to Ford from Germany where he urged Ford to invest in the future of Germany's motor car industry. He said he could not believe Ford would "abandon Germany and leave the task to his Jew competitors, the General Motors people."[12]

Canadian journalists were especially outraged by Ford's anti-British attitudes and his refusal to support Roosevelt's Lend Lease program. One suggested imposing a 10 percent import tax on Ford products, since not to treat him like a foreigner would be rewarding Nazism at home. The author of the piece modified an old poem slamming Ford; it now read:

> Enough for us whose heart
>   hath learned to scorn

Nazis alike, wherever they
   were born;
Who loathe the venom whence
   soe'er it springs,
From Fords or Hitlers, pastry
   cooks or kings.[13]

Ford workers were also writing lyrics during this time. Ford and his army of service department men were fighting unionization bitterly, a battle he lost in 1940 when his employees voted 72,000 strong for union representation and only 2,000 against. Support for the Allies was strong in the U.A.W.-C.I.O. and the organization called for investigations of what they characterized as Ford's "Nazi sympathies." The lyrics to one of their songs go:

But I wonder if those up in heaven
Ever look down from above
And see guns, tear gas, and nightsticks,
A symbol of Ford's brand of love.[14]

If all of this exposure were not enough, Henry Ford began to spout off more to reporters. In 1939, for example, he was asked his opinion of Hitler. Ford said, "I don't know Hitler personally. But at least Germany keeps its people at work." He added, "Apparently England's reason for going to war is that she doesn't make enough use of her land."[15]

The following year an article appeared under his name in *Scribner's Commentator,* a significant event in itself, for this publication was frequently accused of being blatantly pro-Nazi. Its editor, Ralph Townsend, was eventually sent to prison for being an unregistered Japanese agent, and the publication was accused by a federal grand jury of promoting sedition and disunity within the armed forces. Ford's *Scribner's Commentator* article concluded that the Europeans were "duped by the greedy financial groups, seeking to extend their domination over people and lust for power in every branch of human endeavor. These groups are the real 'dictators.'"[16]

In 1941, with Hitler's army now in complete control of the European continent and threatening England's survival, Ford became even more vocal. He raved against the Jews to a *Manchester Guardian* reporter, who later said, "The best he would say about the Jews was that you couldn't do without them. The gentiles wouldn't work if the Jews weren't here." In another interview, this one with the Associated Press, Ford said that the United States should give England and the Axis powers "the tools to keep on fighting until they both collapse." And Ford insisted that any suggestion that the United States would be attacked if Germany won the European war was "pure nonsense, a hoax with the sole purpose of getting us into war."[17]

It is true that by 1941, Ford's support for Hitler seems to have waned. In his biography, Harry Bennett says Ford broke with Hitler when he didn't stop after taking Poland. "Well, by God," he told Bennett, "we're through with him [Hitler]. He's just power drunk like the rest of them." On another occasion, Ford said to a friend, "Do you really want to get rid of Hitler? I'll send Harry [Bennett] over there with six of his men. They'll get rid of Hitler for you in no time."[18] Even in the *Scribner's Commentator* article, Ford showed surprising disrespect for the Fascist leaders when he said, "Certainly no thinking individual believes Hitler and Mussolini represent the real aims and desires of their people. They are puppets upon whom somebody is playing a dirty trick." It was left to the reader to surmise who might be pulling the strings.

Whether Ford lost faith in Hitler is not nearly as important as the fact that he continued to prescribe and promote the Nazi party line in America. Gaining support for racially based fascism was only a part of the Nazi propaganda goal, the lesser part. Germany's higher objective was to encourage isolationism in America. The plotters in Berlin reasoned correctly that they could not take on the United States while in the process of consolidating continental Europe and preparing to invade Britain. In 1940, for instance, the head of Nazi activity in America sent an urgent message to the Reich for funds. He needed $3,000 immediately for a Republican congressman who was rounding up fifty more isolationist congressmen to attend the Republican nominating convention. He also asked for $30,000 for full-page newspaper ads with the message "Keep America Out of the War." The money was sent immediately.[19]

Ford was a staunch isolationist. That was not, of course, through any influence of the Nazi regime. Ford was espousing isolationism long before World War I. The German objective was merely to encourage and exploit Ford's natural predilections and to convince him that Hitler had no ambitions beyond Europe. Ford was convinced. "Hitler wouldn't dare attack us," he said repeatedly. "We have no business in foreign conflicts."[20] To this end, Ford promoted isolationist organizations. Nazi sympathizers also supported these same efforts. The No Foreign Wars Committee had Henry Ford's backing. It also was supported by William Rhodes Davis, a wealthy oil man with major investments in Nazi Germany. When this group came apart at the seams because of rumors of Nazi leanings, Ford backed a new group with many of the same people involved. It was the People's Campaign Against War. The tenets of the organization included defeating aid-to-Britain legislation, preventing Ameri-

can warships from convoying British cargo vessels, and supporting all antiwar congressmen.[21]

Aligned with him in his isolationism was Ford's young
friend, the national hero Charles A. Lindbergh. Ford and Lindbergh first met in 1927, shortly after Lindy's historic trans-
Atlantic flight. Lindbergh came to Dearborn and gave both
Henry and Edsel a ride in the *Spirit of St. Louis*. Charles and
Henry hit it off immediately. They had much in common. They
were both puritanical about their Protestantism, both nonsmok-
ers and nondrinkers, and both great admirers of the efficiency of
the German regime. Both moralists, they believed in common
that sinister forces were undermining the essence of Americanism. Lindbergh, later joined by his brilliant wife Anne Morrow, became close friends with the Fords, often staying at Ford's
Fair Lane mansion. In 1937, Ford expressed his admiration for
Lindbergh by sponsoring a tenth-anniversary celebration of his
flight. When the war broke out, Lindbergh would come to work
for Ford at Willow Run.[22]

Lindbergh and his wife made several lengthy tours of Europe
and were particularly impressed with Hitler's Germany. William Shirer in his *Berlin Diary* tells how the Nazis, led by
Hermann Goering, made a tremendous effort to influence the
Lindberghs during their 1936 visit. Shirer concluded, "The talk
is that the Lindberghs were favorably impressed by what the
Nazis have shown them."[23] On yet another trip to Germany in
1938, Lindbergh wrote in his diary that he was convinced the
German people felt "ashamed of the lawlessness and disorder" of
recent government attacks against Jews. But he was also certain
that the German people believed Jews were "largely responsible
for the international collapse and revolution" following World
War I. [24]

Lindbergh, like Ford, was anti-British. He believed the British were foolish in declaring war on all-powerful Germany and that they, in turn, were attempting to draw America into the conflict to save their necks. As Britain's forces showed strength against the Germans, Lindbergh showed ever-increasing annoyance at them for not surrendering. He once wrote to a friend that "America's encouragement" of the English has complicated "the readjustment that had to take place in Europe." The world, Lindbergh was convinced, could live without Britain and could live with a totally Nazi European continent. "By 1938 I had come to the conclusion," Lindbergh said, "that if a war occurred between Germany on the one side and England and France on the other, it would result in either German victory or in a prostrate and devastated Europe. I therefore advocate that England and France permit Germany to expand eastward into Russia without declaring war."[25]

Any idea of the United States successfully fighting Germany's war machine was absurd to Lindbergh. In a 1941 speech he stated, "If we intend to invade Europe in opposition to the same army and air force that broke the Maginot Line and broke the British forces in Norway, Flanders, and Greece, then the United States must become a military nation. For many years to come we must become a regimented nation . . . that surpasses Germany herself in totalitarian efficiency. In that case we must all realize our way of life is a thing of the past."[26]

Anne Morrow Lindbergh wrote a curious little book which expressed her own and her husband's feelings about the European situation. She said that if Germany had had "reasonable territorial and economic concessions . . . there would have been no Nazism and no war." On the rise of Fascism and Nazism, she asked if it were barbarism, "or is some new, and perhaps even

ultimate good, conception of humanity trying to come to birth."
She, like her husband, said that Germany and Italy had done a
better job of meeting the hunger of their people than the democracies. And her conclusion was, like her husband's and Ford's, "I
do not believe we need to be defended against a mechanized
German army invading our shores, as much as against the decay,
weakness, and blindness into which all the 'democracies' have
fallen since the last war."[27]

Of the Jews, Lindbergh's anti-Semitism was generally more
guarded than Ford's—until 1941, when in a speech he proclaimed, "The three most important groups which have been
pressing this country toward war are the British, the Jews, and
the Roosevelt administration." The Jews' greatest threat to this
country, Lindbergh said, "lies in their large ownership and
influence in our motion pictures, our press, our radio and our
government. . . . Instead of agitating for war, the Jewish groups
in this country should be opposing it in every possible way, for
they will be among the first to feel its consequences."[28]

Lindbergh's anti-Semitism could have been lifted verbatim
out of the pages of the *Dearborn Independent*. His admiration
for Ford undoubtedly had its influence. Yet there may be a
deeper and far more personal reason as well. The Lindberghs'
baby was kidnapped and eventually killed in 1932. Grief over the
death forced the Lindberghs into seclusion for several years. An
unemployed carpenter of German origin, Bruno Hauptmann,
was finally tried and convicted in the case, yet the Lindberghs
found it difficult to believe that the kidnapping could have been
the work of a single individual. They continued to suspect a plot.
In 1935, Julius Streicher wrote for a Nazi American newspaper
that the Lindbergh baby was murdered as part of a Jewish world
plot.[29] The account was widely published at the time. That

Lindbergh saw this accusation is likely; that it influenced his thinking in the midst of his personal grief can only be conjectured.

Whatever his reasons for isolationism and anti-Semitism, he was clearly the darling of the Nazi movement. In John Roy Carlson's book on his undercover work among American Nazis, he notes that Lindbergh's name was invoked freely in those circles. The German-American Vocational League reprinted Lindbergh's articles. Many mistakenly believed that he was one of them, a leader in the movement.[30] Hitler's military attaché in America, General Boetticher, sent numerous messages to the fatherland, painting Lindbergh as a hero. At one point, Boetticher wrote that Lindbergh "now tries at least to impede the fatal control of American policy by Jews. . . . I have repeatedly reported on the mean and vicious campaign against Lindbergh, whom the Jews fear as their most potent adversary." Boetticher also cautioned the German government against openly praising the flyer in the German press because Lindbergh would be accused of being a vassal of Germany. Nonetheless, Hitler awarded Charles Lindbergh the Service Cross of the Order of the German Eagle, with star, one of the highest honors of the Nazi government—of only slightly less stature than the medal Henry Ford had received. Lindbergh kept his award, too. President Roosevelt, who feared Lindbergh's popularity and opposition to his administration, called him a "defeatist and an appeaser." Shortly thereafter, Lindbergh resigned his commission as a colonel in the U.S. Army Air Corps. The resignation was accepted.[31]

Lindbergh's and Ford's names were invariably yoked together during their isolationist phase, partly because of their mutual support but primarily because of their pro-Nazi leanings. Men like Robert Sherwood, two-time Pulitzer Prize winner, called them the "bootlicks of Hitler." This link between the two men was even more apparent when Lindbergh and Ford joined forces and followings in what was to become the most powerful isolationist organization in existence between September 1940 and America's entry into the war after December 7, 1941. The America First Committee began as a group of American blue bloods who were ideologically opposed to war. They were by and large white Anglo-Saxon Protestants of middle age and upper income. They included some of the most influential names in the business and intellectual communities. The committee was, as Carlson said, as "American as Plymouth Rock."

That soon changed. Charles and Anne Lindbergh joined and set out on a massive effort to recruit more members. They succeeded by swelling the ranks from 300,000 to more than 800,000 at the movement's zenith. Unfortunately, the new membership proved surprising to the founders. Henry and Clara Ford joined at Lindbergh's personal encouragement. Soon, America First had some old and familiar names, including Father Charles Coughlin, Reverend Gerald L. K. Smith, Elizabeth Dilling, Reverend Gerald Winrod, William Pelley, Fritz Kuhn, and William Cameron.[32]

The word went out to every pro-Nazi organization in America to join the America First Committee. Father Coughlin told his followers to join for "the one grand objective of keeping this country out of the war." The Ku Klux Klan, Christian Mobilizers, National Workers League, and Silver Shirts were all "instructed" to join. Laura Ingalls was told by her Gestapo agent that "the best you can do is to support America First." Carlson said that attendance at regular Bund meetings suddenly dropped as the transition to America First was in process. To all of this the Nazi government added from Berlin, "The America First Committee is known as true Americanism and true patriotism."

The number of American Bund and Nazi agents who infiltrated America First was astounding. Nazi finance agent Werner C. von Clemm became a financial agent for the group. Nazi agent George Viereck developed propaganda for the committee. Agent Frank Burch became the head of the Akron, Ohio, chapter; and Ralph Townsend, *Scribner's Commentator* editor and Japanese agent, was a frequent spokesman for America First. The organization also had a large number of women's auxiliary groups, with such names as Mothers of Sons Forum, We the Mothers, Loyal American Mothers, National Legion of Mothers, American Women Against Communism, and United Mothers. Chief spokesperson for the women's auxiliary was Laura Ingalls, a known Nazi agent.[33]

Lindbergh became the most vocal spokesman for the committee, while Ford, seventy-eight years old and recovering from a mild stroke, stayed in the background. Michael Sayers and Albert Kahn, in their book *Plot Against the Peace*, tell of an America First rally in Philadelphia in which Lindbergh denounced President Roosevelt and his foreign policies. As he did, the crowd, composed heavily of American Bund and Christian Fronters, became frantic in their applause. "What are we waiting for?" came the shouts. "Are we going to let the Jews run this country?" Sayers and Kahn say that in the excitement of the moment, members of the audience forgot themselves and jumped to their feet, giving the Nazi straight-arm salute.[34]

The America First Committee became openly anti-Semitic. The *Protocols* were being sold at committee gatherings. At one meeting, Mrs. Geraldine Buchanan Parker sang out the theme,

"Your literature does not need to state the word 'Jew.' All you have to do is accuse the international bankers. The masses have now been educated to understand what is meant."[35] The prospect of impending war seemed linked to the Jews in the minds of these isolationists.

Garland Alderman, former secretary of the pro-Nazi National Workers' League and America First Committee member, later admitted, "I wanted to keep America out of war, and thought I could do it better by spreading anti-Semitism."[36]

If war was declared, the Jews "will be among the first to feel its consequences," Lindbergh had said, mouthing the implied threat that ran throughout the America First approach. It was clear that many leading Jews were behind President Roosevelt and anxious, because of the obvious personal threat Hitler posed to them, not to compromise with the Nazi regime. One typical accusatory article, this one by Frank C. Hanighen, said, "Jews are solidly organized against isolationism in a 'downright unJewish manner.'"[37] So the anti-Semites who had chosen the Jew as their collective scapegoat were now admonishing him for not being passive enough. As Senator Gerald Ney, a leading isolationist, put it, "I wish that those who would be its victims would sense the possibilities."[38]

The original members of the America First Committee attempted unsuccessfully to regain their organization. They pointed out that Henry Ford was a rabid anti-Semite and asked him to resign. He complied, but by then the ranks were so thoroughly saturated with anti-Semitism that it was too late. Finally, on September 11, 1941, Lindbergh alienated the remaining leading members of the old guard in a speech delivered in Des Moines, Iowa, in which he all but accused American Jews of attempting to force this country into war. The Jews were for the war, Lindbergh contended, because of the persecution of the Jews in Germany. "We cannot blame them for looking out for what they believe to be their own interests," he said, "but we also must look out for ours. We cannot allow the natural passions and prejudices of other peoples to lead our country to destruction."[39] Membership of those who were not pro-Nazi plummeted from that moment on.

Whether America First was falling apart on its own accord is of little importance, for within three months of Lindbergh's Des Moines speech, the organization was disbanded. Japan attacked Pearl Harbor, and Germany, Italy, and Japan declared war on the United States, doing exactly what Lindbergh and Ford had said would never happen. Lindbergh, however, had his final say. At the farewell dinner of the America First Committee twelve days after war was declared, Lindbergh told his audience that the real cause of the world's problems was the British, and that Germany and the United States ought to be fighting together against Communists and the "yellow hordes."[40]

Shortly afterward, failing to regain his Air Corps commission, Lindbergh returned to Michigan to work for Henry Ford. Announcing Lindbergh's arrival in Detroit as if he were a conquering hero was Reverend Gerald L. K. Smith, who wrote, "The presence of Lindbergh in Detroit is one of the most inspiring events to take place since Pearl Harbor. The youthfulness of America's hero, alongside the wisdom of America's industrial sage, serves notice on the world that real Americanism still is, and real Americans are, still alive."[41]

War changed the complexion of Ford Motor Company almost overnight. As he had done at the outset of World War I, Henry Ford immediately set aside his isolationism in favor of military production. Within months, the Ford Willow Run Plant would

131

be producing B-24 bombers, and all Ford plants would soon convert to making arms and machinery of war. Ford Motor Company became one of the major producers for the War Department. This was largely due to Edsel Ford and Charles Sorenson, who, seeing the war on the horizon, made frequent trips to Washington, D.C., to work out defense contracts before Pearl Harbor.

Henry was now nearly eighty years old and, with two strokes behind him, his memory was weakening. That didn't mean that the company president, Edsel Ford, now had command. His father still insisted on making the final decisions, yet in his weakened condition, he turned more and more to Harry Bennett to speak for him. "There wouldn't be anything left if it wasn't for Harry," Ford said in 1942. "The Jews and Communists have been working on poor Harry until he's almost out of his mind."[42]

Since Bennett neither knew nor cared anything about manufacturing, the situation was at best chaotic. Edsel Ford, Sorenson, and Bennett each attempted to run their own operations. It was understood, however, that Bennett could have the upper hand in any dispute if he chose to exercise his close connection to Henry, Senior.

The old man's failing health, however, did allow Edsel and young Henry Ford II to attempt to cope with the disastrous public image the senior Ford had fostered through twenty years of anti-Semitism. It perhaps speaks well for the American public's common sense that none of the ploys used by Ford during the 1930s to present himself as a reformed friend of the Jews had worked. Polls conducted by Ford Motor Company at Edsel's direction in 1940, and again in 1942, showed that more than 78 percent of the American male public had heard that Ford was anti-Semitic. An Elmo Roper study in 1944 came to the conclusion that Ford had so thoroughly alienated American Jews that they had all but completely stopped buying the company's cars and trucks in the late thirties. If the company was going to be in the car business after the war ended, it was obvious something would have to be done to improve the Ford image.

As early as 1941, Edsel Ford designated large amounts of money for advertising in the Yiddish and English-language Jewish press. The total amount spent on these advertisements is not known, but there are records of the expenditure of nearly $84,000 in Jewish publications in 1943 alone—a year when the company was not even selling cars. Edsel also set up a special fund of $50,000 for local sales promotions to be used by regional managers in areas like New York and Chicago with significant Jewish populations.[43]

The company finally attempted to fulfill its promise of 1927 by stopping publication of the *International Jew* wherever possible. Gerald L. K. Smith issued the book in 1941 and was promptly met by a statement from Henry Ford II, grandson of Old Henry and newest member of the family to enter the company. Young Henry disavowed any sponsorship of the book. "The publication of this book is entirely without the sanction, authorization, or approval of Mr. Henry Ford, the Ford Motor Company, or myself," he said. At the same time he announced the policy of the company and the family to "urge all American citizens to combat any movement . . . to foster . . . prejudice against any group."[44]

Now Edsel and Henry II moved to stop other uses of the family name in connection with the *International Jew*. Company lawyers threatened the Ku Klux Klan with a major lawsuit unless they stopped circulating the book in Ford's name. Imperial Klan

Wizard J. A. Colescott agreed to cease distribution. Mexican, Central American, and South American governments also received strong pleas from the Ford Motor Company to investigate and stop publication of the book. The effort worked—at least in removing the Ford name. The Anti-Defamation League reported in 1945 that a search of ten Latin American countries revealed no copies of the *International Jew* on public sale. The league credited the achievement to the efforts of the Ford Motor Company.[45]

Richard Gutstadt, Director of the Anti-Defamation League, was also called upon to draft a letter of good will to the Jewish people which would appear over Henry Ford's name. He did so; Edsel and his public relations men went over it; and this time it went out with Henry Ford's actual signature. The letter read:

> In our present national and international emergency, I consider it of importance that I clarify some general misconceptions concerning my attitude toward my fellow-citizens of the Jewish faith. I do not subscribe to or support, directly or indirectly, any agitation which would promote antagonism against my Jewish fellow-citizens. I consider that the hate-mongering prevalent for some time in this country against the Jew, is of distinct disservice to our country, and to the peace and welfare of humanity.
>
> At the time of the retraction by me of certain publications concerning the Jewish people, in pursuance of which I ceased [sic] the literature prepared by certain persons connected with its publication. Since that time I have given no permission or sanction to anyone to use my name as sponsoring any such publication, or being the accredited author thereof.
>
> I am convinced that there is no greater dereliction among the Jews than there is among any other class of citizens. I am con-

vinced, further, that agitation for the creation of hate against the Jew or any other racial or religious group, has been utilized to divide our American community and to weaken our national unity.

I strongly urge all my fellow-citizens to give no aid to any movement whose purpose it is to arouse hatred against any group. It is my sincere hope that now in this country and throughout the world, when this war is finished and peace once more established, hatred of the Jew, commonly known as anti-Semitism, and hatred against any other racial or religious group, shall cease for all time.[46]

The letter had little impact and received minimal attention and commentary in the general press. Ford, after all, had made similar statements before, only to follow them up with contradictory comments and actions. Few believed that Henry Ford was any more honest in this letter than he had been in the 1927 retraction or the Franklin letter in 1938. In retrospect, Edsel Ford's signature would have carried more credibility. He, after all, had never expressed the anti-Semitic notions of his father, and many knew that Edsel had often disagreed with the old man over the issue. It would have been Edsel's one chance to publicly announce his own position. For Edsel had inoperable cancer, related to the stomach ulcer he had suffered for years retaining his silence working under his dictatorial father. The following spring, Edsel Ford died. He was forty-nine years old. His father, in much improved health, attended the funeral without shedding a tear.

Edsel's death worried the War Production Board. Without the stability of the son, and grandson Henry II now away in Navy boot camp, having volunteered for service, it seemed as if there was no Ford they could trust at the helm of a family-owned business. Henry assumed the presidency of the company, but that didn't dispell the concern in Washington. Finally, at the board's urging, Henry Ford II, not yet twenty-six years old, was released from the service and sent back to Dearborn to join the company as vice-president.

Young Henry's arrival in Dearborn was hardly thought to bode well. He was a pudgy and pampered young man who had never shown a great deal of promise. As a youth he was a practical joker, delighting in visiting the plant and taking all the workers' time cards out of the rack, shuffling them up, then putting them back. As a boy in private school, his teacher recalls Henry "was not notable for his intellectual brilliance."[47] And he had to leave Yale for allegedly cheating on his final examinations. He seemed hardly equal to the task of organizing a company which had no structured management, little bookkeeping, and no tools and equipment of recent vintage. Nor was Old Henry willing to turn over the reigns of power. In fact, he had even begun to talk about willing the presidency of the company to Harry Bennett. All bets were that the company would soon go under through sheer internal chaos.

That did not happen, of course. Henry Ford II managed to gain control, with the help of his mother and grandmother. The young Ford then cleaned out the old guard, starting with Harry Bennett and ending with Ernest Liebold. The reign of anti-Semitism within Ford Motor Company was ended. The Flivver King had abdicated.

Henry Ford continued on as before, working a full day when his health would permit, which was most days. He no doubt heard about Gerald L. K. Smith, Gerald Winrod, Elizabeth Dilling, and others who continued their racist programs throughout the war, more often than not blaming "the Jew war machinery" for the world's dilemma.[48] Ford said nothing. At the close of the war, he may have heard about Dr. Robert Ley's letter to him from the prison at Nuremberg. Dr. Ley, chief of the German Labor Front and a rabid anti-Semite, wrote to Ford asking for a job as soon as the trials were over.[49] Days later, Ley hanged himself in his cell. Ford had not responded.

Ford was to suffer another major stroke in May of 1945. Josephine Gomon, in her unpublished manuscript, "Poor Mr. Ford," tells how the stroke came about. Ms. Gomon was a personal friend of Ford and Bennett, and worked for them as the first woman executive of the company during World War II. She has also been called an architect of the New Deal, and was the director of Detroit's first low-income housing development. As Ms. Gomon relates the story, Henry Ford went to the Rouge plant auditorium to watch the first uncut films of the Nazi atrocities in the Majdanek liquidation camp. Ford suffered his most severe stroke as he watched the films. "He never recovered his mind or physical strength," Gomon says.[50] Henry Ford died the following February. Neither Ford Motor Company nor the Ford Archives can either confirm or deny Gomon's account of the stroke. At the time, the stroke was downplayed because of the defense contracts. Yet if Gomon's story is true, and considering her credentials there is no reason to believe it is not, then Ford may have come to realize the ultimate outcome of the hatred he had helped project onto an entire people. He may have seen and felt what he could never, with his mechanic's limited imagination, have envisioned himself.

As for Ford's anti-Semitic writings, they live on in various forms today. In the 1960s, both Gerald Smith and the John Birch Society reprinted parts of Ford's version of the *Protocols*. Smith serialized most of the *International Jew* in his magazine. In the 1970s, the American Neo-Nazis and Arab groups have taken up Ford's "improved" version of the *Protocols*.

How long can it last? Perhaps the best prediction came when Henry Ford II in 1947 again publicly reiterated that neither Ford Motor Company nor he sanctioned the latest printing of the *International Jew*. The *Canadian Jewish Review* concluded that Henry Ford II "was doing something which he probably will be called on to do at intervals during his whole life because his grandfather unloosed an evil which will not be cleaned up in the grandson's time."[51]

7

Why,
Henry?
•

HENRY Ford is an enigma. Here is a man who, at the height of his career, was a farsighted humanist, and who had gained the highest respect and wealth his country could bestow. How he could have become such an ardent anti-Semite and fascist poses difficult problems for anyone attempting a rational analysis. Even Adolf Hitler's insane program of anti-Semitism can be explained—in its initial stage—as a pragmatic ploy. Hitler had much to gain by developing the image of an evil force corrupting the "pure Aryan nation." The German people could feel exempt from their failures in war and in peacetime economics. In "the Asiatic Jew," Hitler found a rallying point for nationalism, based not on arbitrary borders, but on "race." Henry Ford had no such motive for his anti-Semitism. In a fundamentally tolerant society, Ford's fanaticism created only problems for himself and his family. To attack an American ethnic group meant the

139

expenditure of millions of dollars and the loss of perhaps hundreds of millions, considering the number of potential car buyers—Jew and non-Jew alike—whom he alienated during a half century.

A number of historians and biographers have suggested reasons for Henry Ford's anti-Semitism. They are often quick, glib answers that the rational mind can understand, categorize, and set aside. Yet each fails when juxtaposed against Ford's complex, and often contradictory, personality.

The most common conclusion, for example, is that Ford was the pawn of sinister men working for him. Gomon blames Liebold and Cameron. Liebold blames Bennett. Others say all three manipulated the billionaire industrialist. The anti-Semitism, many conclude, seems to emanate not from Ford but from one or more of these men—which is exactly how Henry wanted it to look.

The truth is that no one ever controlled Ford. He was, by the accounts of those who were closest to him, as near to an absolute dictator in his realm as could be imagined. Every important decision made within the Ford Motor Company during his long tenure was made by Ford himself, most of the time based on a hunch or pure gut feeling.[1] If anyone disagreed, he was either fired or, as in the case of his own son, simply ignored. Biographer William Richards confirms that "no executive was so secure that he could do what Ford did not want done."[2]

Ford, however, had no stomach for arguments or for doing the dirty work of firing or smearing a man. For that he retained men like Liebold and Cameron. They survived precisely because they did not oppose Ford, but carried out his wishes without question. That group includes the violent Harry Bennett, who never once raised his voice to his boss. As Charles Sorenson testified in

My Forty Years with Ford, "Bennett did not control Henry Ford, the reverse was true."[3] This is not to say that these men did not encourage Ford's anti-Semitism, but it was more a matter of forever finding out what Mr. Ford wanted to hear, then giving it to him without qualification. Had Liebold, Cameron, and Bennett walked out in moral indignation, there is little question that Ford would have found others to perform the same functions. The image of the gentle rustic being manipulated by a host of Rasputins is an apologist's argument which does an injustice to Ford's strength of will.

Edwin Pipp, the first editor of the *Dearborn Independent,* who walked out rather than continue to publish lies about the Jews, contends that Ford's anti-Semitism sprang from Ernest Liebold but was sustained through political ambitions. While Ford was running for the Senate, it would be to his advantage to be anti-Semitic, since he could gain the support of Ku Klux Klansmen and work on the rural prejudices in Michigan, which was then predominantly farm country. That also explains why Ford retracted his statement in 1927, according to Pipp; Ford was then eyeing the presidency of the United States, and the politics involved would be different. Ford came to the realization, Pipp says, that when the United States elects a president, the votes are not cast directly for the candidate, but for 531 presidential electors who do the final choosing. New York and Ohio, as we have already noted, had large Jewish populations, and it was a fact that "since 1856, a period of sixty-six years in which sixteen presidential elections took place, every candidate who lost both Ohio and New York lost the election."[4]

The logical question one would ask, if this were true, is why Ford continued to have his men distribute anti-Semitic material if he seriously feared losing the Jewish vote? Pipp's answer is that "the very nature of the man would lead him not to let anyone [for which read "the Jews"] have his own way entirely."[5]

The flaw in this argument is that Ford did not actually covet the office of president. He appears to have used his candidacy as a threat against the administration, hoping to obtain Coolidge's support for the Muscle Shoals deal if he would back out. The ploy seems to have worked. Moreover, the political-ambitions theory does not explain Ford's continued anti-Semitism throughout the remainder of his life. Whatever Ford's reasons, he was anti-Semitic to the pith of his soul and did not conjure it up in himself, as others did in the 1930s, for sheer financial or political gain.

Nor was he motivated by any negative experience in the financial world, as some contended. According to the stories, Ford had attempted to borrow $20,000 from New York Jewish banking houses during a difficult period of the company's history.[6] They allegedly treated him poorly and turned down his loan application. From this, one was to conclude that Ford decided that the Jew bankers were plotting against gentiles. This story has no basis in fact. Ford was never turned down for a loan by Jewish bankers; in fact, he had little dealing with bankers of any sort throughout his career.

Another source has it that what actually happened is that Ford went to a Jewish bank in New York to cash a check from Europe and was ushered upstairs where he found "a lot of Jews sitting around smoking cigars as long as chimneys."[7] They infuriated him by taking a great deal of time to cash the foreign check. Thus, international banking, Jews, and smoking all fit into the same tale.

One documented incident of conflict between Ford and Jewish financiers is in his attempt to purchase the Detroit, Toledo &

142

Ironton Railroad. The firm of Tannenbaum and Strauss refused to sell its shares, which kept Ford from gaining the total control he demanded in all of the businesses he took over.[8] The tenacity of these Jewish businessmen no doubt disturbed him. Yet none of these experiences and tales seems significant enough to have turned Ford to anti-Semitism. He had numerous business transactions over the years, mostly with gentiles, and did not always get the better of the deal. But these are weak foundations for a multimillion-dollar attack against an entire people.

Why not, then, simply take Henry Ford at his word? According to Ford, he became convinced of the international Jewish conspiracy during his Peace Ship experience in the winter of 1915. The episode began when Madame Rosika Schwimmer, a Hungarian Jew, approached Ernest Liebold in Dearborn to gain an audience with the industrialist. She had read in the papers that Ford was against the war and would give his entire fortune to combat the spirit of militarism that pervaded America at that time. Schwimmer was a strong and determined woman, a campaigner for birth control and woman suffrage as well as immediate peace. She met with Henry and Clara Ford and convinced them both to act against the war, suggesting that they overwhelm President Wilson with telegrams demanding that the United States stop flirting with the allies and act to end hostilities. Ford agreed to spend $10,000 for the project. But before the plan could be announced, an interviewer misquoted Ford and greatly expanded the original idea into proposing a Peace Ship which would sail for Europe and force the negotiations.

The trip turned out to be a fiasco. Thomas Edison refused to accompany him, even though Ford said he would give Edison $1 million to go along. Soon after the ship set sail, Ford was drenched by a wave while jogging on deck, and he spent most of the trip in his berth with a serious cold and in the ship's engine compartment, where he felt at home amid the machinery. There was constant bickering on board between Schwimmer, who assumed command during Ford's illness, and members of the press. Ford later recalled to Liebold that this experience was "a monkey show." As soon as they docked in Norway, Ford left the group. He talked to reporters four days later, not about peace, but of his new tractor soon to go on sale. Soon after, he quietly caught a ship back to America and considered the entire episode finished, even though it had cost him nearly half a million dollars.

Unfortunately, Ford left Schwimmer in Europe to carry on without funds. Two weeks later she complained to the press from Sweden that she was "ill and in want" and had received no support whatsoever from Henry Ford. She managed to continue working for the establishment of peace talks for several more months; then she went home to Hungary where she was appointed a minister to Switzerland, an unprecedented high position for a woman in that era. Soon she was asked to resign the post because she had spent too much government money on the trappings of the office, which to her included a fur coat, chauffeured limousine, and an elegant apartment.[9]

Six years after the Peace Ship incident, during Christmas, 1921, Henry Ford told a *New York Times* reporter in Florence, Alabama:

> It was the Jews themselves who convinced me of the direct relationship between the international Jew and war. In fact, they went out of their way to convince me.
>
> On the peace ship were two very prominent Jews. We had not been at sea 200 miles before they began telling me of the power of

144

the Jewish race, of how they controlled the world through their control of gold, and that the Jew and no one but the Jew could end the war. I was reluctant to believe it but they went into detail to convince me of the means by which the Jews controlled the war, how they had the money, how they had cornered all the basic materials, needed to fight the war and all that, and they talked so long and so well that they convinced me.

They said, and they believed, that the Jews started the war, that they would continue it as long as they wished, and that until the Jew stopped the war it could not be stopped. I was so disgusted I would have liked to turn the ship back.[10]

The press immediately dug out accounts of the Peace Ship and concluded that the individual who soured Henry Ford on the Jews must have been Rosika Schwimmer. Ford, however, denied this. He said Mme. Schwimmer was more intelligent than the lot of the people aboard ship put together. Years later, Ford came to her defense when others blamed her for his bias.[11]

The following February when New York writer and editor Herman Bernstein published a book exposing the *Protocols* as absolute lies, Henry Ford said that it was Bernstein, a journalist and fellow voyager on the Peace Ship, who had told him all about the Jews. Ford claimed that Bernstein said the war would not end until the international Jews were ready for it to end. He also said other newspaper correspondents confirmed Bernstein's accusations after Ford arrived in Norway. Outraged, Bernstein denied the charge and filed a $200,000 libel suit against Ford. Ford withdrew his accusation, made a public apology to Bernstein, and settled the case out of court.[12]

For those who would take Henry Ford at his word, the Peace Ship statement settled the problem of how he became an anti-

Semite. Ford, however, habitually invented stories of his past to justify his current positions. It is worth nothing that he made his Peace Ship statement after he had run the first ninety-one anti-Semitic articles in the *Dearborn Independent* and when the opposition to his publication was at a high point. If Ford's story is true, then the inevitable question is, why did he wait six years to tell it? Ford's personality was such that he would more likely have told the press about what he had learned within days of the experience.

While it is possible that Bernstein, a socialist, may have spoken out against the international money interests who were profiting from the war, his outspoken opposition in print to the *Protocols* and other Jewish-plot concepts makes it highly improbable that he would have implicated Jews as warmongers. The best analysis of Ford's thinking comes from Rosika Schwimmer herself. Burnet Hershey, in his book *The Odyssey of Henry Ford and the Great Peace Ship,* tells of an interview he had with Mme. Schwimmer in which she said that Ford was infected with anti-Semitism long before he met her. During their first meeting in Dearborn, Schwimmer says, Ford proclaimed he knew who caused war—"International Jews." He added, "I have the evidence here—facts! I can't give them out yet because I haven't got them all. I'll have them soon."[13]

Ford's Jew mania is far too complex to have been inspired by a single traumatic event or by the negative impact of a single strong personality like Mme. Schwimmer. Rather, it appears to be the outcome of broad social forces and numerous events acting in concert upon Ford's unsophisticated mind. He was a man whose heaviest adult reading was the newspaper and the *Reader's Digest,* whose favorite book of all time was *Bambi.*[14] He did not understand the sociological forces of the age, yet he consumed the essence of their undercurrents, and reacted violently to them.

At the time of Henry Ford's birth in 1863, for example, there were fewer than a quarter million Jews in all of America. Detroit had a population of 400 Jews out of a total community of 53,000. And rural Dearborn had one Jewish family. The nation's history was a blank sheet on the subject of Jew baiting, and the Jews of the American Revolution had fought in Washington's army and contributed heavily to the financial needs of the revolutionary cause.[15]

What Jews there were in Henry Ford's world were primarily German and Reform and differed little in manners and customs from the large German Lutheran population in Detroit. In 1867, the environment in southeastern Michigan was such that Isaac Mayer Wise wrote that Detroit's Jews "live in the best understanding and harmony with their neighbors and are esteemed as men, citizens, and merchants."[16]

In the one-room schoolhouse where Ford received his primary education, he had no Jewish peers. Yet he did have the image of the Jew presented in McGuffey's readers, which Henry idolized. The image found expression in Dickens's Fagin and in Shakespeare's Shylock.[17] The Jew, in the popular agrarian mind, though tolerated, was assumed to be somehow less than Christian in morals and business ethics.

Occasionally, such sentiments would flare up, as in the year Ford was born when a Detroit publication accused the Jews of being Civil War profiteers. They are, the article said, "the tribe of gold speculators who are doing their best to create distrust of the government," adding that these "hooked-nosed wretches speculate on disasters, and a battle lost to our army is chuckled over by them, as it puts money in their purse."[18] Such sentiments, how-

147

ever, were the exception that served only to point out the underpinning of anti-Semitism which the first- and second-generation immigrants brought with them from Europe.

Two phenomena beginning in Henry Ford's teenage years altered the relatively tranquil relationships between Jews and gentiles in America. First, there was the Populist movement which swept across the Grain Belt and centered on the fears and frustrations of farmers like Henry Ford and his father. In 1878, the Central Greenback Club of Detroit announced that the economic collapse following the Civil War and the railroad scandals of the day were laid to "the Rothschilds across the water." Wall Street was depicted in editorial cartoons as a massive Jewish pawnshop. The gold standard was depicted as the ultimate evil, and the Jew was somehow assumed to be the cause of it.[19]

In the Populist model, the quintessential American was a man who worked with his hands. The antithesis was the man who manipulated ideas and money—the financier, the creditor who makes his living "at the expense" of the toil of "real Americans." Not only financiers, but anyone who did not labor by hand was suspect, which, of course, created mistrust of all business people and academics. To the extent that the early influx of Spanish, German, and Polish Jews were proponderantly either merchants or scholars, the Jew exemplified all that which the Populist considered evil.[20]

In Populist thinking we find all of the fundamentals of Ford's economic anti-Semitism. It was a childish assumption which linked all finance to Jewry. This explains his sister's argument that Henry was not really anti-Semitic; "he called all the moneylenders of the world 'Jews' regardless of their religion."[21] Mme. Schwimmer would agree. Her personal assumption after years of reflecting on Henry Ford was that "his was a unique form of economic anti-Semitism, like his hatred of Wall Street. He regards Wall Street as the ogre within the ranks of capital, as a thorn between national and foreign wealth."[22]

The second major event which influenced Ford's thinking occurred when an anarchist dropped a bomb into the lap of Tsar Alexander II in 1881. His son, Alexander III, blamed the Jews and set out to rid his country of them through pogroms, conversion to Christianity, and forced emigration. What followed was a mass exodus of Jews from Russia and Poland to the United States. Jews were resented all the more in Eastern Europe because of the tremendous increase in their population since 1800, mainly due to reduction in the infant death rate through improvements in medicine and sanitation. The numbers were astounding. Between 1880 and 1910, more than 2 million Jews would migrate to America. The rapid influx led one professor to predict that within 100 years the United States would be inhabited primarily by Slavs, Negroes, and Jews.[23]

The influx caused a xenophobic reaction. For the new arrivals were not only coming in record numbers, they were far different from the Jews that Americans of longer standing had known until then. These were Orthodox Jews with customs, dress, and mannerisms alien to the Americans of West European background.

They were all the more visible because they tended to mass together in major cities and to enter a few occupations to which entry was easiest, quickly surpassing in the fields they chose. The Russian Jew came with an ambition that was startling to most other Americans. They would not only put in more hours at a trade, they would innovate techniques that earned them advantages. The "team" idea in garment making was an excellent example. Instead of the cottage-industry approach that the Ger-

149

mans had been using, Jews introduced assembly-line methods. A Jewish tailor, for example, might contract with garment companies to make large quantities of a single item. The mother would cut out the patterns; brothers and sisters, aunts and uncles would each do one sewing task over and over again; and the father might oversee the production and help anyone who fell behind. This kind of productivity frightened members of other ethnic groups who feared for their jobs.

Jews also came with a passion for higher learning which upset still more native Americans. The urban system of education, particularly in New York City, made it possible for poor immigrant children to go through college at little cost. Rural Americans, on the other hand, usually had to leave home to have access to postsecondary education. The Jews, more than any other immigrant group, took full advantage of free public schooling. By 1907, when Jews constituted about 25 percent of the population of New York City, they were the largest single ethnic group in the public schools. Jews were entering professional schools in such large numbers that Lawrence Lowell of Harvard imposed a quota, limiting Jewish enrollment there.[24]

These developments inspired a rash of anti-Semitism which continued to grow until 1924 when the passage of restrictive immigration laws successfully stopped the Jewish exodus to America. During these years open anti-Semitism was everywhere. Newspapers carried ads for jobs which specifically stated "Christians Only Need Apply." Private clubs of all kinds and professional organizations sprang up which refused to allow Jewish members. Jewish peddlers were often attacked in the streets by gangs of teenagers. While the harassment and discrimination against the Jews never reached anything comparable to a Russian pogrom, it was nonetheless a seriously unsettling time for most Jewish Americans.[25]

During most of these years, Henry Ford lived and worked in Detroit. He had watched the population of Jews grow from 1,000 in 1880 to 10,300 in 1900 and to 34,000 in 1914. Robert Rockaway, in perhaps the only comprehensive survey of anti-Semitism in Detroit during that period, reports of the widely voiced fear of the "threatening tide." Jews were accused of being a health menace and a threat to Christian traditions. At least one minister preached that they were a "pauper and lawless class." Rockaway documents the presidential campaign in 1896 in which a float was paraded through Detroit depicting a giant pawnship of Isaac Silberstein with "men representing the wandering Jew auctioning off all kinds of secondhand goods." Discrimination against Jews in business clubs, such as the Detroit Athletic Club, was common. All of which prompted Dr. Leo Franklin to sigh that "Jews are tolerated, not welcomed."[26]

Ford could not have helped but be aware of these radical changes. His anti-Semitic writings certainly show a fear of what he perceived to be the Jewish invasion. And he must also have been influenced by those about him reacting to the "Asiatic Jews." Ironically, Dr. Franklin may even have inadvertently contributed to Ford's anti-Semitic view. Franklin, like many German Jews in Detroit at the time, urged the incoming Jews not to organize or do other things which would further set them apart from the mainstream Americans. "There can be no political organization among Jews as Jews," Franklin said in 1902. "Those among us who attempt to unite the two [religion and political organization] are neither Jews nor Americans."[27] Franklin criticized the "few scalawags among us" who would give the non-Jew the wrong idea about Jewish separatism. Since Franklin was Henry Ford's next-door neighbor and personal friend during that period, it is likely that this subject was discussed. Ford may have felt that Franklin would welcome his

151

criticism of those who Ford thought would make America Jewish rather than make Jews Americans. That may explain Ford's genuine surprise when Dr. Franklin objected to his first articles attacking the Jews in the *Dearborn Independent*.

Another reaction to the large-scale immigration was the development of organizations and ideologies to protect the purity of the "Aryan race." The concept, of course, derived from an obsession among some Germans with Teutonic bloodlines, but it was largely ignored in America until the wave of immigration appeared to some to pose a threat to the native stock. Writers such as Lothrop Stoddard and Grant Madison gained large followings in the United States in the years around World War I preaching Nordic racism. Ford accepted these notions, which were eventually expressed in the *Dearborn Independent*'s defense of the "Anglo-Saxon-Celtic race. . . . they are the ruling people, chosen throughout the centuries to master the world."[28]

These factors certainly made their impressions on Henry Ford, but none of them did as much to shape his concepts as his lifelong idol and friend, Thomas Alva Edison. "He was the chief hero of my boyhood, and he became my friend in manhood." Ford said. "I hold him to be our greatest American."[29] Ford's reverence for Edison assumed religious proportions. They first met in 1898 at a banquet where Edison showed interest in the young inventor's gasoline carriage and encouraged him to go on. It was, by Ford's account, "the first encouraging word I ever had from any informed person."[30] Edison at first disliked Ford, but eventually they became close friends. Ford built a house next door to Edison's in Fort Myers, Florida, to be able to visit him. Ford lent Edison millions of dollars over the years of their friendship. Ford bylined a book about him. He enshrined Edison by building the Edison Institute as part of the Greenfield

Village complex in Dearborn, Michigan. He brought Edison's entire cluster of buildings from Menlo Park, his first laboratory, plus an acre of New Jersey clay, to Dearborn. And after Edison's death in 1931, Ford's most treasured possession was a glass bottle he kept in a shoebox labeled "Edison's last breath."[31]

Superficially, the two men seemed to have much in common despite the sixteen-year difference in their ages. Both were raised in rural Michigan, both were absolute believers in hard work and trial-and-error learning, both had a closer relationship with their mothers than with their fathers, and both were absolutely against the evils of tobacco. The differences were actually far greater than their similarities, however. Thomas Edison was a thoroughly self-educated man of whom it was said there was no subject on which he could not be conversant. He was also a thoroughly practical man. Both characteristics were in sharp contrast to Ford's romanticism and lack of education. Edison, however, admired Ford for his ability to make money, something Edison never seemed to be able to do well.[32] Ford admired Edison as a father figure, seeking his advice and, with few exceptions, carrying it through. It was Edison, for example, who told Ford to stay out of the Automobile Manufacturers Association and to fight the Selden Patent. Ford took the advice and won the suit. In all the nearly forty years of their friendship, Edison always called Ford "Henry," while he never called the wizard of Menlo Park anything but "Mr. Edison."[33]

The relationship is important because it represents the strongest influence anyone ever had over Henry Ford, with the possible exception of his wife Clara. Edison's views, his expectations and his prejudices, became Henry Ford's.

Edison, for example, was absolutely against the gold standard. In his view, the best basis for evaluating money was the energy resources of a country. As a young adult in 1870, Edison was for the Greenbackers, who amassed half again as many votes in Michigan as the Republican party that year. Ford, too, became a Greenbacker.[34]

Edison was against unionism, believing that the struggle between worker and employer was a natural process that must occur. Ford became antiunion.

Edison, above all, hated Wall Street. He did not trust the financiers, whom he saw as a corrupting force in society. One of Edison's greatest disappointments was the secret merger that lost him Edison General Electric and the dropping of his name from the new corporate logo. Ford became a Wall Street hater.[35]

Was Edison also anti-Semitic? There are some indications that he was. Edison told a *Detroit Journal* reporter in 1914 that the rise of commerce in Germany fostered the war, and that Jews were responsible for Germany's business success. He added that he believed the military government to be a pawn of the Jewish business sector. Within two weeks, however, Edison wrote to Herman Bernstein saying that he had been badly misquoted. What he actually had said was, "If one went down to the bottom of things in the great and most successful industries, one would dip up a Jew who furnished the ability to make them a success."[36]

During the series of anti-Semitic articles appearing in the *Dearborn Independent,* Edison gave indications of support for that effort. On December 1920, for instance, Edison corresponded with Liebold on the anti-Semitic articles, saying that "they don't like publicity." On several other occasions he sent notes that implied at least tacit support, and in a note dated November 28, 1924, Edison sent Liebold a news clipping entitled "Jews are Ruling Soviet Russia," which stated that out of the forty-eight leaders of the Soviet government, only five were of pure Russian blood. Edison's attached note says only, "Liebold: This is interesting. Edison."[37] Moreover, Ford send Edison a complete set of volumes of the *International Jew*, in a special leather presentation binding. Edison graciously accepted with "thanks."

The evidence on Edison's anti-Semitism is far from conclusive. It is known that he employed Jews in his laboratory and, except for the few notes to Liebold in his late seventies, never made an anti-Semitic comment to anyone. Also, we have the testimony of Harry Bennett, who said that "more than once I heard Edison rebuke Mr. Ford for his prejudice. Mr. Ford always denied it to him."[38]

Was he or wasn't he? The evidence seems to indicate that Edison shared the Populist notion that Wall Street was dominated by Jews, and it was the Jews in the financial professions whom Edison resented. Edison could have applauded the first articles pointing a finger at Jewish international bankers; but, as the articles continued, it is doubtful that he could have accepted the bizarre accusations.

There are some indications that Edison encouraged Ford to drop the anti-Semitic series. For one, Ford said that his reason for stopping the attack was to bring down the gold standard. The gold standard was Edison's obsession during these years. In his eulogy of Edison in 1931, Ford said: "Latterly he [Edison] turned his mind to economic questions because he believed the present system hindered the best in men. . . . He was convinced that our money machinery was badly in need of attention."[39] If Edison was anti-Semitic, as his notes to Ford indicate, then it appears to be the unique form of the disease to which Mme. Schwimmer refers in Ford's case—economic anti-Semitism.

Yet another strong influence on Ford's anti-Semitism is a little-noticed lifelong friend, Dr. Edward A. Rumely. The two men first shared an interest in developing farm tractors and other methods of mechanizing agriculture. They corresponded frequently between 1908 and 1910 on the subject and visited each other several times at Interlaken and La Porte in western Michigan.[40] Throughout the 1920s, Dr. Rumely was an independent financial consultant to Ford. He had great influence with the magnate. In 1926, for example, everyone in the Ford organization including Edsel was urging Henry to come up with a replacement for the outdated Model T. Henry would hear none of it. Yet when Dr. Rumely gave him the same advice, he listened, and eventually agreed.[41] The relationship continued unabated throughout the thirties, judging by the Rumely letters appearing periodically throughout the Ford Archives correspondence files.

Rumely was interested in more than tractors. During World War I he was an active member of the German propaganda establishment. He spent some $200,000 for advertisements in 619 ethnic newspapers in America urging individuals to protest the sending of war supplies to the Allies. With $1.5 million in German government money, Dr. Rumely purchased the *New York Evening Mail*, running it for two years and retaining a pro-German stance. It all caught up with him in July 1918 when he was arrested and charged under the Trading with the Enemy Act. During this time, Henry Ford went to Washington, D.C., to use whatever pull he had with Congress and the administration to help his friend. Dr. Rumely, however, was eventually convicted of the charges but served only one month in prison, receiving a pardon from President Coolidge.[42] During this period, U.S. Ambassador to England George Harvey publicly

156

accused Henry Ford of aid to Rumely's espionage activities during the war.[43]

After his conviction, Dr. Rumely dropped out of the public eye for a decade, yet his name comes up again in connection with the *Dearborn Independent*. Through his friend Henry Ford, he arranged to get a friend of his a propaganda position on the Ford newspaper. The man was Dr. August Muller, a German nationalist who reportedly helped Brasol and Cameron write the *Independent*'s anti-Semitic series and the *International Jew*.[44]

Finally, Dr. Rumely surfaces again in 1937 when he established an organization called the Committee for Constitutional Government, the sole purpose of which was to attack President Roosevelt and counteract his Lend Lease and other programs which were focused against Nazi Germany. John Roy Carlson notes that Dr. Rumely's organization had ties with the rest of the anti-Semitic and pro-German gang of the period, including Elizabeth Dilling and Father Coughlin's Christian Front.[45] Rumely's "patriotic" organization lasted until 1944, during which time he spent an estimated $2 million on antiwar and anti-Roosevelt ventures.

How much influence Dr. Rumely had on Henry Ford is hard to say. But his involvement with Ford before and during World War I may well explain part of Ford's attitude toward Germany and the Jews at the end of the hostilities.

This still does not explain the great lengths and expense Ford went to in attacking the Jews. There were many men of his era who were fundamentally prejudiced, yet only Ford was so obsessed by the Jewish threat as to feel the need to wage open hostilities. The answer seems to lie in a series of failures in Ford's life which nurtured his paranoia.

World War I was Ford's first major defeat. He was character

ized as a fool for his pacifism at a time when the overwhelming sentiment of the American people was to enter the war. Ford told the press that the American flag was a "tribal emblem" and parrotted Samuel Johnson that "patriotism is the last refuge of a scoundrel."[46] He created so many hard feelings that even after the war began and Ford turned immediately to making arms, members of the press and government continued to attack him. Former President Theodore Roosevelt expressed a typical reaction when he said, "Mr. Ford has been given immensely valuable war contracts of the government. No doubt he has executed them as well as the thousands of other contractors who now render service to government for pay, but no service he can thus render the government can offset the frightful damage he did our people by the lavish use he made of his enormous wealth in a gigantic and profoundly anti-American propaganda against preparedness and against our performance of international duty during the two and a half years before we entered the war."[47]

The Peace Ship episode was the crowning failure of his antiwar efforts. Again he was publicly humiliated. Ford could not understand why anyone would be against his desire for peace—unless, of course, there were money interests at stake.

Next came his defeat for a seat in the U.S. Senate. His opponent's attacks on the pacificism issue, and on Edsel Ford's deferment from the military service, must have struck at his fragile ego. Newberry spent a great deal of money on the campaign, as did Liebold on Ford's behalf, but in Ford's mind, Newbold's financing meant that he must be getting backing from New York money men. When Ford lost, he was convinced that the Jews had made a fool of him.[48]

The ultimate humiliation came with the *Chicago Tribune* libel suit. Again, it was tied to Ford's antiwar efforts. In 1916,

158

President Wilson had asked for volunteers to join the army to fight Mexican bandits. Knowing Ford's sentiments on war, a *Chicago Tribune* reporter called the company and asked if employees going to war would have a job when they came back. A spokesman for the company answered no without checking with Ford first. Truth was, Ford's policy was to guarantee every such employee a job upon return. The *Chicago Tribune* then attacked Ford, and the lawsuit was instituted, finally going to court in the summer of 1919.[49]

On the witness stand and in front of a packed gallery of journalists, Ford was repeatedly made to look like an uneducated fool. As the pressure wore on, he began to show his feelings of persecution. In one exchange, for instance, he was being asked about a reporter who, Ford claimed, misquoted him after an interview. The reporter, Ford said, "did not look free." The opposition attorney asked if Ford meant the reporter looked like a slave. "Yes, a slave to the financiers," Ford answered. "I think he was trying to trap me into saying things."[50]

More than one of Ford's biographers has observed that the *Chicago Tribune* trial scarred his personality and tinged his mind with wariness, bitterness, and cynicism. The financiers had beaten him again, he concluded, this time by using their prestige to control the press. Remember that his beating at the hands of the press took place during the same summer that he first received the *Protocols* from Brasol. And the *Protocols* states that "through the press we have gained the power to influence while remaining ourselves in the shade."[51]

Finally, there was the Bolshevik revolution, which set off suspicions and conspiracy accusations that make the McCarthy era of the 1950s look gentle in comparison. In the first five months after the World War I armistice, Charles Merz notes, 387 articles appeared about Bolshevik activities in the *New York Times* alone.[52] The "proof" that Jews led the revolution in Russia was the final evidence that Ford's persecution complex needed. The difficulties he had experienced, the wars in Europe and Russia, and all of the corruptions he had seen since moving to the city had to be the work of financial conspirators. Once his eye was jaundiced, he looked at other competitors to see Jew financiers. General Motors had become a pawn of the Du Ponts, he felt, and the treasurers were Jews. Chrysler was a stock company, therefore a creation of Wall Street. His fear of financiers became such that he would allow only the barest minimum of accounting within his company and even fired the entire accounting department once because they asked for more office space. Banks were not to be trusted, either. Ford must have lost millions of dollars in interest over the years by keeping large sums of cash on hand. At one point, he even suggested that he might bury his profits rather than trust a bank.

Norman Hapgood, the *Hearst's International* writer who exposed many of Ford's anti-Semitic activities during the 1920s, concluded that away from his assembly plant, Ford's mind was that of a child."[53] And like a child, he lived in a fanciful world of his own creation. He had good guys—mainly himself, his yes men, and the Germans—and the villains—Jews, Catholics, smokers, and drinkers. Reasoning was just so much talk to a man who lived only by hunches and feelings. Since he did not trust the press, he could hardly be expected to believe their reports of the inhumanities Jews were suffering under Hitler in the late 1930s. He lived just long enough to hear the tally of at least 4 million Jews exterminated and to see the films of bodies piled two stories deep. If he felt any remorse for his contribution, we have no idea, for Henry Ford never spoke of the Jews again.

If we are to take any consolation from the story of Henry Ford, it is that, despite his colossal wealth and heroic stature, he was never able to turn the majority of Americans toward anti-Semitism. The rise of anti-Semitism from 1890 through 1930 was primarily the result of xenophobia, an emotional reaction against the millions arriving in those years. By 1935 the dozens of anti-Semitic groups were already largely ineffectual. A major poll that year showed that even in the Midwest, the traditional hotbed of prejudice, 84 percent of the population was against anti-Semitism as practiced under the Hitler regime.[54]

That is not to say that the Holocaust could never happen here. The Leo Frank case in 1915[55] and the blood libel incident at Massena, New York, in 1928[56] certainly prove that it is possible for anti-Semitic prejudice even when held by only a minority of a community, to lead to hysteria and violence. The Henry Ford experience adds yet another dimension. Theodore Roosevelt characterized Ford as "ignorant, yet because he has been so successful in motors, many, many persons, hardly as ignorant as himself, think him wise in all things, and allow him to influence their views."[57]

One has only to read through the letters of encouragement in the Ford Archives—letters from otherwise compassionate people condemning the Jews, letters from numerous Christian ministers praising the anti-Semitic attacks and enclosing money for copies of the *International Jew*, letters from college professor and illiterate alike—to be impressed by how easily people would believe Ford about ethnic hatred and politics, simply because he made a car that pleased them.

Had Henry Ford not been such a timid soul, had he been able

to face microphones and crowds, he might very well have been elected President of the United States, despite his already well-established prejudices. It is not too farfetched to suggest that all that stood between Ford and the power of our highest office was the lack of a Dale Carnegie course in public speaking—and that is a sobering thought to be left with.

Notes

•

1.   An American Folk Hero

[1] William Simonds, *Edison: His Life, His Work, His Genius* (New York: Blue Ribbon Books, 1952), p. 313.

[2] Reynold M. Wik, *Henry Ford and Grass-Roots America* (Ann Arbor, Mich.: University of Michigan Press, 1973), p. 6; and Allan Nevins and Frank Ernest Hill, *Ford: Decline and Rebirth* (New York: Charles Scribner's Sons, 1963), pp. 120-121.

[3] Booton Herndon, *Ford: An Unconventional Biography of the Men and Their Times* (New York: Weybright & Talley, 1969), p. 387.

[4] Upton Sinclair, *The Flivver King* (Detroit: United Auto Workers of America, 1937), p. 22; and Herndon, *Ford: An Unconventional Biography,* p. 147.

[5] William C. Richards, *The Last Billionaire: Henry Ford* (New York: Charles Scribner's Sons, 1948), pp. 12-14.

[6] Allan Nevins and Frank Ernest Hill, *Ford: Expansion and Challenge* (New York: Charles Scribner's Sons, 1958), p. 606.

[7] Henry Ford, *My Life and Work* (Garden City, N.Y.: Garden City Publishing Co., 1922), p. 3.

[8] James Brough, *The Ford Dynasty: An American Story* (Garden City, N.Y.: Doubleday & Co., 1977), p. 76.

[9] Herndon, *Ford,* p. 136.

[10] Wik, *Henry Ford and Grass-Roots America,* p. 9.

[11] Propaganda Analysis Institute, untitled booklet, July 1938, p. 3.

[12] Ford, *My Life and Work,* p. 40.

[13] "Henry Ford at Bay," *The Forum Magazine,* August 1919, p. 143.

[14] Propaganda Analysis Institute booklet, p. 3.

[15] Keith Sward, *The Legend of Henry Ford* (Toronto: Rinehart & Co., 1948), pp. 89-93.

[16] Brough, *The Ford Dynasty,* pp. 31-45.

[17] Margaret Ford Ruddiman, *Memoirs of My Brother Henry Ford* (Lansing, Mich.: Michigan Historical Commission, 1953), pp. 243-244.

[18] Brough, *Ford Dynasty,* p. 53.

[19] Brough, *Ford Dynasty,* pp. 100-103; and Nevins and Hill, *Ford: Expansion and Challenge,* pp. 70-75.

[20] Richards, *The Last Billionaire,* p. 145.

[21] Herndon, *Ford,* pp. 366-367.

[22] John B. Rae, *Great Lives Observed: Henry Ford* (Englewood Cliffs, N.J.: Prentice-Hall, 1969), p. 152.

[23] Rae, *Great Lives Observed,* pp. 163-168; Brough, *Ford Dynasty,* pp. 107-109; and "Henry Ford at Bay," pp. 129-143.

[24] Samuel Marquis, *Henry Ford: An Interpretation* (New York: Little, Brown & Company, 1923), p. 51.

[25] Spencer Ervin, *Henry Ford vs. Truman H. Newberry* (New York: Richard R. Smith, 1935; Anne Jardin, *The First Henry Ford: A Study in Personality and Business Leadership* (Cambridge, Mass.: The M.I.T. Press, 1970), pp. 135-139; and Sward, *The Legend of Henry Ford,* pp. 116-125.

[26] John Kenneth Galbraith, *The Liberal Hour* (New York: Houghton Mifflin Company, 1960), p. 155.

2.   The Truth According to Ford

[1] Ford Archives, Restricted Box 199.

[2] James Brough, *The Ford Dynasty: An American Story* (Garden City, N.Y.; Doubleday & Co., 1977), p. 117.

[3] William C. Richards, *The Last Billionaire: Henry Ford* (New York: Charles Scribner's Sons, 1958), p. 90.

[4] *PM* magazine, August 14, 1940.

[5] James and Suzanne Pool, *Who Financed Hitler: The Secret Funding of Hitler's Rise to Power 1919-1933* (New York: The Dial Press, 1978), p. 89; and Keith Sward, *The Legend of Henry Ford* (Toronto: Rinehart and Co., 1948), p. 143.

[6] Ford Archives, Accession 285, Box 609.

[7] Allan Nevins and Frank Ernest Hill, *Ford: Decline and Rebirth* (New York: Charles Scribner's Sons, 1963), p. 124.

[8] Sward, *Legend of Henry Ford,* p. 141.

[9] *The American,* January 10, 1919.

[10] Sward, *Legend,* p. 142.

[11] David Lewis, *The Public Image of Henry Ford* (Detroit: Wayne State University Press, 1976), p. 136.

[12] Ford Archives, *Dearborn Independent* papers.

[13] Ford Archives, Liebold's Reminiscences, p. 441.

[14] Louis Ferdinand, Prince of Prussia, *The Rebel Prince* (Chicago: Henry Regnery Company, 1952), p. 154.

[15] Allan Nevins and Frank Ernest Hill, *Ford: Expansion and Challenge* (New York: Charles Scribner's Sons, 1958), p. 314.

[16] Philip Slomovitz interview, *Detroit Jewish News,* September 20, 1979.

[17] Sward, *Legend,* p. 148.

[18] Ford Archives, Accession Box 6-256, Edwin Pipp speech before Temple Israel, Akron, Ohio, April 5, 1921.

[19] Nevins and Hill, *Ford: Expansion and Challenge,* p. 314.

[20] Sward, *Legend,* p. 147.

[21] Ford Archives, Liebold's Reminiscences, p. 450.

[22] Ferdinand, *The Rebel Prince,* p. 154.

[23] Richards, *The Last Billionaire,* p. 280.

[24] Sward, *Legend,* p. 137.

[25] Norman Hapgood, in *Hearst's International,* August 1922.

[26] Ford Archives, Black's Reminiscences.

[27] Harry Bennett, as told to Paul Marcus, *We Never Called Him Henry* (New York: Fawcett Books, 1951), p. 47.

[28] Ford Archives, Liebold papers, Accession 64.

[29] Ibid.

[30] Norman Hapgood in *Hearst's International*, July 1922.

[31] Ibid.

[32] American Jewish Archives, letter from Casimir Palmer to Prof. Nathan Isaacs, March 25, 1933.

[33] John Roy Carlson, *Under Cover: My Four Years in the Nazi Underworld of America* (New York: E. P. Dutton, 1943), p. 204.

[34] *Jewish Examiner*, August 25, 1939.

[35] Ralph Lord Roy, *Apostles of Discord* (Boston: Beacon Press, 1953), pp. 42-44.

[36] Hugo Valentin, *Antisemitism: Historically and Critically Examined* (New York: The Viking Press, 1936), p. 183.

[37] Ibid., p. 165.

[38] Ford Archives, Liebold's Reminiscences, p. 465.

[39] John Spargo, *The Jew and American Ideals* (New York: Harper and Brothers, 1921), p. 7.

168

[40] Based on an overall reading of *Dearborn Independents,* May 1920-October 1922.

[41] Ford Archives, Liebold's Reminiscences.

[42] Sward, *Legend,* p. 193.

[43] Ford Archives, Harold Hicks' Reminiscences, p. 178.

[44] Richards, *Last Billionaire,* p. 95.

[45] Henry Ford, *My Life and Work,* (Garden City, N.Y.: Garden City Publishing Co., 1922), p. 241.

[46] James Martin Miller, *The Amazing Story of Henry Ford, the Ideal American and World's Most Famous Private Citizen* (Chicago: M. A. Donahue & Co., 1922), p. 139.

[47] Nevins and Hill, *Ford: Decline and Rebirth,* p. 315.

[48] Richards, *Last Billionaire,* p. 95.

[49] Ford Archives, Liebold's Reminiscences, p. 458.

[50] Bennett, *We Never Called Him Henry,* p. 47.

[51] *New York Times,* April 2, 1921.

[52] Lewis, *Public Image of Henry Ford,* p. 141.

[53] Ford Archives, Liebold's Reminiscences, p. 446.

⁵⁴ Nevins and Hill, *Ford: Expansion and Challenge,* p. 315.

⁵⁵ Pool and Pool, *Who Financed Hitler,* p. 87.

⁵⁶ Rabbi Lee J. Levinger, *Anti-Semitism in the United States* (Westport, Conn.: Greenwood Press, 1972), p. 97.

⁵⁷ Ford Archives, Accession 62, Box 100.

⁵⁸ *New York Times,* January 6, 1922.

⁵⁹ Lewis, *Public Image,* p. 142.

⁶⁰ Charles Reznikoff, ed., *Louis Marshall: Champion of Liberty* (Philadelphia: Jewish Publication Society of America, 1957), pp. 341-347.

⁶¹ Lewis, *Public Image,* p. 140.

⁶² Pool and Pool, *Who Financed Hitler,* p. 88.

⁶³ Ford Archives, Accession 285, Box 126.

⁶⁴ Ford Archives, Accession 62, Box 100.

⁶⁵ Anne Jardin, *The First Henry Ford: A Study in Personality and Business Leadership* (Cambridge, Mass.: The M.I.T. Press, 1970), p. 145.

⁶⁶ *Friday* magazine, January 24, 1941.

⁶⁷ *Sioux City News,* September 30, 1921.

[68] Ford Archives, *Dearborn Independent* Correspondence, November 2, 1921.

[69] Levinger, *Anti-Semitism in the United States,* p. 79.

[70] Based on a general reading of correspondence, 1920-1924.

[71] Richards, *Last Billionaire,* p. 96.

[72] Upton Sinclair, *The Flivver King* (Detroit: United Automobile Workers of America, 1937), p. 59.

[73] Lewis, *Public Image,* p. 211.

[74] Ibid., p. 212.

3. Hitler's Inspiration

[1] David Lewis, *The Public Image of Henry Ford,* (Detroit: Wayne State University Press, 1976), p. 143.

[2] Keith Sward, *The Legend of Henry Ford,* (Toronto: Rinehart & Co., 1948), p. 160.

[3] *Chicago Tribune,* March 8, 1923.

[4] *Detroit News,* December 31, 1931.

[5] William C. Richards, *The Last Billionaire: Henry Ford,* (New York: Charles Scribner's Sons, 1948), p. 13.

6 *New York Times,* February 10, 1924.

7 Louis Ferdinand, Prince of Prussia, *The Rebel Prince,* (Chicago: Henry Regnery Company, 1952), p. 155.

8 Norman Cohn, *Warrant for Genocide,* (New York: Harper & Row, Publishers, 1966), p. 160; John Roy Carlson, *Under Cover: My Four Years in the Nazi Underworld of America,* (New York: E. P. Dutton, 1943), p. 477; and Michael Sayers and Albert Kahn, *The Plot Against the Peace,* (New York: The Dial Press, 1945), pp. 229-231.

9 Ford Archives, Liebold's personal papers.

10 Saul S. Friedman, *The Incident at Massena,* (New York: Stein & Day Publishers, 1978), p. 93.

11 American Jewish Archives, Nathan Isaacs' letters from Casimir Palmer, March 25, 1933.

12 Ibid., letter of March 29, 1933.

13 Resulting from numerous inclusions in *The International Jew,* vols. I-IV, (Dearborn, Mich.: The Dearborn Publishing Co., 1920).

14 *International Jew,* vol. III, no. lxi.

15 Joachim C. Fest, *Hitler,* (New York: Harcourt Brace Jovanovich, 1973), p. 91.

16 *New York Evening Journal,* September 25, 1936.

[17] *International Jew,* vol. IV, no. lxxiv.

[18] *Chicago Tribune,* March 8, 1923.

[19] Lewis, *The Public Image,* p. 90.

[20] Carlson, *Under Cover,* p. 205.

[21] Ford Archives, *Dearborn Independent* restricted box.

[22] Ford Archives, Liebold's Reminiscences, p. 471.

[23] William L. Shirer, *Berlin Diary,* (New York: Alfred A. Knopf, 1943), p. 149; Lewis, *Public Image,* p. 143.

[24] Konrad Heiden, *A History of National Socialism,* (New York: Octagon Books, 1971), p. 109.

[25] *New York Times,* December 20, 1922.

[26] Alton Frye, *Nazi Germany and the American Hemisphere,* (New Haven, Conn.: Yale University Press, 1967), p. 172.

[27] James and Suzanne Pool, *Who Financed Hitler? The Secret Funding of Hitler's Rise to Power 1919-1933,* (New York: The Dial Press, 1978), p. 113.

[28] Ford Archives, Liebold's personal papers.

[29] Upton Sinclair, *The Flivver King,* (Detroit: United Automobile Workers of America, 1937), p. 109.

[30] George Seldes, *Facts and Fascism* (New York: In Fact, Inc., 1943), p. 122.

[31] *New York Times*, December 10, 1922.

[32] *New York Daily Worker*, August 16, 1939.

[33] Konrad Heiden, *Hitler: A Biography*, (New York: Alfred A. Knopf, 1936), p. 221.

[34] Kurt G. W. Lüdecke, *I Knew Hitler*, (New York: Charles Scribner's Sons, 1937), pp. 264-265.

[35] Frye, *Nazi Germany*, pp. 172-173.

[36] *Time*, June 1, 1970; and Elizabethe Corathiel, ed., *Oberammergau Passion Play*, (Westminster, Md.: Newman Press, 1960), selected readings.

[37] *Detroit Free Press*, March 3, 1923; *New York Times*, April 20, 1929 and August 13, 1975; and *The People's Almanac*, vol. I, (Garden City, N.Y.: Doubleday & Co., 1975), pp. 1296-1298.

[38] Pool and Pool, *Who Financed Hitler*, pp. 112-130.

[39] Hajo Holborn, *Republic to Reich: The Making of the Nazi Revolution*, (New York: Pantheon Books, 1972), p. 346.

[40] Dietrich Eckart, *Der Bolschewismus von Moses bis Lenin: Zwiegespraech Zwischen Adolf Hitler und Mir (Bolshevism from Moses to*

Lenin: A Dialogue Between Adolf Hitler and Myself, (Munich: Hoheneichen Verlag, 1924), p. 247.

[41] Fest, *Hitler,* p. 200.

[42] James Brough, *The Ford Dynasty: An American Story,* (Garden City, N.Y.: Doubleday & Co., 1977), p. 257.

[43] Louis Ferdinand, *The Rebel Prince,* p. 155.

[44] The parallels that follow are taken from detailed comparisons between Henry Ford's *International Jew,* vols. I-IV, and Adolf Hitler's *Mein Kampf,* (New York: Hurst and Blackett, 1939).

[45] Vamberto Morais, *A Short History of Anti-Semitism,* (New York: W. W. Norton & Co., 1976), p. 203.

[46] P. G. J. Pulzer, *The Rise of Political Anti-Semitism in Germany and Austria,* (New York: John Wiley & Sons, 1964), p. 326.

4. Ford Re-Tractor

[1] James Brough, *The Ford Dynasty: An American Story,* (Garden City, N.Y.: Doubleday & Co., 1977), p. 147.

[2] *Dearborn Independent,* April 12, 1924.

[3] Ford Archives, Accession 48, Box 39.

[4] Ibid.

[5] *New York Times,* April 2, 1927.

[6] *Dearborn Independent,* January 31, 1925.

[7] Charles Reznikoff, ed., *Louis Marshall: Champion of Liberty,* (Philadelphia: Jewish Publication Society of America, 1957), p. 372.

[8] Reynold M. Wik, *Henry Ford and Grass-Roots America,* (Ann Arbor, Mich.: University of Michigan Press, 1973), p. 136.

[9] Ford Archives, *Dearborn Independent,* business receipts.

[10] *New York Times,* April 1, 1927.

[11] Ibid., April 23, 1927.

[12] Keith Sward, *The Legend of Henry Ford,* (Toronto: Rinehart & Co., 1948), p. 152.

[13] *New York World,* April 4, 1927; and Allan Nevins and Frank Ernest Hill, *Ford: Expansion and Challenge,* (New York: Charles Scribner's Sons, 1948), pp. 317-320.

[14] William C. Richards, *The Last Billionaire: Henry Ford,* (New York: Charles Scribner's Sons, 1948), p. 98.

[15] Anne Jardin, *The First Henry Ford: A Study in Personality and Business Leadership,* (Cambridge, Mass.: The M.I.T. Press, 1970), p. 145.

[16] Ford Archives, Liebold's Reminiscences, p. 456.

176

[17] *Detroit News* and *New York Times*, April 1-10, 1927.

[18] American Jewish Archives, general anti-Semitic files.

[19] *New York Times*, April 10, 1927.

[20] Nevins and Hill, *Ford: Expansion and Challenge*, p. 319; and Brough, *The Ford Dynasty*, pp. 171-172.

[21] David Lewis, *The Public Image of Henry Ford*, (Detroit: Wayne State University Press, 1976), pp. 145-146.

[22] Richards, *The Last Billionaire*, p. 99.

[23] *Detroit News* and *Detroit Free Press*, April 7-12, 1927.

[24] Harry Bennett, as told to Paul Marcus, *We Never Called Him Henry*, (New York: Fawcett Books, 1951), p. 53.

[25] *New York Times*, April 21, 1927.

[26] Bennett, *We Never Called Him Henry*, p. 56.

[27] Reznikoff, *Louis Marshall*, p. 380

[28] *New York Times* and *Detroit News*, July 8, 1927.

[29] *New York Times*, July 26, 1927.

[30] *Dearborn Independent*, July 30, 1927.

[31] *New York Times,* July 8, 1927.

[32] Detroit Public Library, National Automotive Historical Collection.

[33] John Cote Dahlinger, *Secret Life of Henry Ford,* (New York: The Bobbs-Merrill Co., 1978), p. 107.

[34] Consolidation of wide selection of readings between July 8 and September 1, 1927.

[35] *Society of Automotive Engineers Journal,* February 1929, pp. 111-114.

[36] Richards, *Last Billionaire,* p. 101.

5. The Friendly Puppeteer

[1] David Lewis, *The Public Image of Henry Ford,* (Detroit: Wayne State University Press, 1976), p. 147.

[2] Charles Reznikoff, ed., Louis Marshall: Champion of Liberty, (Philadelphia: Jewish Publication Society of America, 1957), p. 388.

[3] Kurt G. W. Lüdecke, *I Knew Hitler,* (New York: Charles Scribner's Sons, 1937), p. 35.

[4] "Fundamental Principles," booklet, (Detroit: Anglo-Saxon Federation, 1928).

[5] *Friday* magazine, April 14, 1940.

[6] *National American,* December 4, 1933.

7 *Saturday Review of Literature,* September 14, 1940.

8 *Ohio Jewish Chronicle,* January 15, 1937.

9 Ford Archives, Accession 285, Box 1769; and Liebold Correspondence.

10 Ford Archives, Accession 285, Box 1769.

11 *The American Hebrew,* December 25, 1936.

12 *New York Times,* January 7, 1937.

13 Donald S. Strong, *Organized Anti-Semitism in America: The Rise of Group Prejudice During the Decade 1930-40,* (Westport, Conn.: Greenwood Press, 1941), p. 15.

14 Nathan C. Belth, *A Promise to Keep: A Narrative of the American Encounter with Anti-Semitism,* (New York: Times Books, 1979), p. 118.

15 *Friday* magazine, April 14, 1940.

16 John Roy Carlson, *Under Cover: My Four Years in the Nazi Underworld of America,* (New York: E. P. Dutton, 1943), pp. 166-170; and Ralph Lord Roy, *Apostles of Discord,* (Boston: Beacon Press, 1953), p. 169.

17 Ford Archives, restricted Box 199, letter from Gutstadt to Bennett, January 2, 1942.

[18] *New Republic,* November 11, 1936; and *American Mercury,* November 1938.

[19] Harry Simonoff, "The First Henry Ford and His Dearborn Independent," (New York: Block Publishing Co., undated pamphlet), American Jewish Archives.

[20] Interview with Philip Slomovitz, Detroit Jewish News, September 1979.

[21] Sander A. Diamond, *The Nazi Movement in the U.S. 1924-1941,* (Ithaca, N.Y.: Cornell University Press, 1974), p. 155.

[22] *PM* magazine, August 14, 1940.

[23] American Jewish Archives, Nathan Isaacs' Collection, letter from Casimir Palmer to Isaacs, May 11, 1937.

[24] *PM* magazine, August 14, 1940.

[25] Strong, *Organized Anti-Semitism in America,* pp. 24-26; Michael Sayers and Albert Kahn, *The Plot Against Peace,* (New York: The Dial Press, 1945), pp. 33-65; and Carlson, *Under Cover,* pp. 111-112.

[26] Ford Archives, Accession 44, Box 17.

[27] Ford Archives, Liebold Papers, August 21, 1937.

[28] Keith Sward, *The Legend of Henry Ford,* (Toronto: Rinehart & Co., 1948), p. 458.

29 *Detroit News,* December 7, 1939.

30 Samuel Marquis, *Henry Ford: An Interpretation,* (New York: Little, Brown & Company, 1923), p. 54; James Brough, *The Ford Dynasty: An American Story,* (Garden City, N.Y.: Doubleday & Co., 1977), pp. 17-163; and Upton Sinclair, *The Flivver King,* (Detroit: United Automobile Workers of America, 1937), pp. 86-87.

31 Harry Bennett, as told to Paul Marcus, *We Never Called Him Henry,* (New York: Fawcett Books, 1951), p. 17.

32 Ford Archives, Accession 64, Liebold Papers.

33 W. M. Cunningham, "J8: A Chronicle of the Neglected Truth About Henry Ford and Ford Motor Company," pamphlet, (Detroit: North American Publishing Co., undated).

34 *In Fact,* July 21, 1941, Archives of Labor History and Urban Affairs, Wayne State University, Detroit.

35 Sward, *Legend of Henry Ford,* p. 337.

36 Interviewed at Detroit, Jewish News, September 1979.

37 *Friday* magazine, February 14, 1941.

38 *PM* magazine, September 20, 1940.

39 *In Fact,* July 21, 1941.

40 *New York Times,* March 21, 1937.

[41] Charles J. Tull, *Father Coughlin and the New Deal*, (Syracuse, N.Y.: Syracuse University Press, 1965), P. 206.

[42] *New Masses*, December 12, 1939.

[43] American Jewish Archives, letter from Charles Coughlin to Casimir Palmer, July 26, 1938.

[44] American Jewish Archives, Isaacs' Collection, letter from Casimir Palmer, November 12, 1938.

[45] *Social Justice*, articles March 13, 1936-January 10, 1941; and Arthur Morse, *While Six Million Died: A Chronicle of American Apathy*, (New York: Random House, 1968), p. 227.

[46] *Look* magazine, September 26, 1939.

[47] Carlson, *Under Cover*, p. 296.

[48] Belth, *A Promise to Keep*, pp. 130-145.

[49] Hal Draper, *The Truth About Gerald Smith, America's No. 1 Fascist*, (Los Angeles: The Worker's Party, 1945), p. 14.

[50] *American Mercury*, August 1942.

[51] Sward, *Legend*, p. 459.

[52] Gerald L. K. Smith, *Matters of Life and Death*, (Los Angeles: Christian National Crusade, 1958), pp. 47-48.

[53] Belth, *Promise,* p. 144.

6. Ford's Final Thrust

[1] *Detroit Free Press,* July 31, 1938; and *New York Herald Tribune,* July 31, 1938, and September 10, 1938.

[2] Ford Archives, Accession Box 64; and David Lewis, *The Public Image of Henry Ford,* (Detroit: Wayne State University Press, 1976), p. 148.

[3] Josephine Fellows Gomon, "Poor Mr. Ford," unpublished manuscript, Bentley Historical Library, Michigan Historical Collection, Ann Arbor, Mich., p. 116.

[4] *Detroit News* and *Detroit Times,* December 2, 1938; and *Detroit News,* December 4, 1938.

[5] *Detroit Free Press* and *New York Daily News,* December 5, 1938.

[6] *PM* magazine, August 14, 1940; and Allan Nevins and Frank Ernest Hill, *Ford: Decline and Rebirth,* (New York: Charles Scribner's Sons, 1963), p. 280.

[7] *PM Sunday,* September 16, 1945.

[8] Michael Sayers and Albert Kahn, *The Plot Against the Peace,* (New York: The Dial Press, 1945), p. 34.

[9] Nevins and Hill, *Ford: Decline and Rebirth,* pp. 176-178.

[10] *PM* magazine, August 14, 1940.

[11] Associated Press, December 28, 1940.

[12] Allan Nevins and Frank Ernest Hill, *Ford: Expansion and Challenge,* (New York: Charles Scribner's Sons, 1958), p. 562.

[13] *Wilton's Review,* July 31, 1940.

[14] Wayne State University, Archives of Labor History, Ford Files.

[15] *Detroit Free Press,* August 29, 1939.

[16] *Scribner's Commentator,* December 1940; John Roy Carlson, *Under Cover: My Four Years in the Nazi Underworld of America,* (New York: E. P. Dutton, 1943), p. 414; and Keith Sward, *The Legend of Henry Ford,* (Toronto: Rinehart & Co., 1948), p. 461.

[17] Associated Press, February 16, 1941.

[18] Harry Bennett, as told to Paul Marcus, *We Never Called Him Henry,* (New York: Fawcett Books, 1951), p. 120.

[19] William L. Shirer, *The Rise and Fall of the Third Reich,* (New York: Simon & Schuster, 1960), p. 748.

[20] Nevins and Hill, *Ford: Decline and Rebirth,* p. 168.

[21] Sayers and Kahn, *Plot Against the Peace,* pp. 188-189; and American Jewish Archives, General Anti-Semitic Files.

184

[22] Leonard Mosley, *Lindbergh: A Biography*, (Garden City, N.Y.: Doubleday & Co., 1976), pp. 315-317; and Nevins and Hill, *Ford: Decline and Rebirth*, pp. 168-174.

[23] William L. Shirer, *Berlin Diary*, (New York: Alfred A. Knopf, 1943), pp. 51-52.

[24] Charles A. Lindbergh, *The Wartime Journal of Charles A. Lindbergh*, (New York: Harcourt Brace Jovanovich, 1970), p. 131.

[25] Sayers and Kahn, *The Plot Against the Peace*, p. 194.

[26] Mosley, *Lindbergh*, pp. 293-312.

[27] Anne Morrow Lindbergh, *The Wave of the Future: Confession of Faith*, (New York: Harcourt, Brace & Co., 1940), pp. 13-15, 33.

[28] *New Republic*, September 22, 1941; and *New York Times*, September 12, 1941.

[29] Sander A. Diamond, *The Nazi Movement in the U.S. 1924-1941*, (Ithaca, N.Y.: Cornell University Press, 1974), p. 158n.

[30] Carlson, *Under Cover*, p. 184.

[31] Alton Frye, *Nazi Germany and the American Hemisphere*, (New Haven, Conn.: Yale University Press, 1967), pp. 148-149; Nevins and Hill, *Ford: Decline and Rebirth*, pp. 181-183; and Mosley, *Lindbergh, pp. 293-303*.

[32] Carlson, *Under Cover*, pp. 185-187 and 331.

185

[33] Sayers and Kahn, *Plot Against the Peace,* pp. 187-193; and Carlson, *Under Cover,* p. 242.

[34] Sayers and Kahn, *Plot,* p. 193.

[35] Ibid., p. 206.

[36] Carlson, *Under Cover,* p. 330.

[37] *Common Sense,* June 1941.

[38] *New Republic,* September 22, 1941.

[39] *New York Times,* September 12, 1941.

[40] Mosley, *Lindbergh,* pp. 308-309.

[41] Carlson, *Under Cover,* p. 506.

[42] Nevins and Hill, *Ford: Decline and Rebirth,* pp. 260-262.

[43] David Lewis, *The Public Image of Henry Ford* (Detroit: Wayne State University Press, 1976), pp. 145-155.

[44] *The Detroit Times,* April 2, 1941.

[45] Lewis, *Public Image,* p. 152.

[46] Nathan C. Belth, *A Promise to Keep: A Narrative of the American Encounter with Anti-Semitism,* (New York: Times Books, 1979), pp. 82-84.

[47] James Brough, *The Ford Dynasty: An American Story*, (Garden City, N.Y.: Doubleday & Co., 1977), pp. 179-251.

[48] Sayers and Kahn, *Plot Against the Peace*, pp. 183-185.

[49] Joe J. Heydecker and Johannes Leeb, *The Nuremberg Trial*, (Westport, Conn.: Greenwood Press, 1958), pp. 85-86. .

[50] Gomon, "Poor Mr. Ford," p. 117.

[51] Lewis, *Public Image*, p. 155.

7. Why, Henry?

[1] Booton Herndon, *Ford: An Unconventional Biography of the Men and Their Times*, (New York: Weybright & Talley, 1969), p. 167.

[2] William C. Richards, *The Last Billionaire: Henry Ford*, (New York: Charles Scribner's Sons, 1948), p. 98.

[3] Charles E. Sorenson, *My Forty Years with Ford*, (New York: W. W. Norton & Co., 1956), p. 256.

[4] Edwin G. Pipp, *The Real Henry Ford: Henry as I Know Him—and I Know Him*, (Detroit: Pipp's Weekly, 1922), pp. 21-28.

[5] Ibid., p. 27.

[6] Charles Merz, *And Then Came Ford*, (Garden City, N.Y.: Doubleday, Doran, & Co., 1929), pp. 184-185.

[7] Richards, *The Last Billionaire*, p. 89.

[8] Allan Nevins and Frank Ernest Hill, *Ford: Expansion and Challenge*, (New York: Charles Scribner's Sons, 1958), p. 312.

[9] James Brough, *The Ford Dynasty: An American Story*, (Garden City, N.Y.: Doubleday & Co., 1977), pp. 21-25; and Allan Nevins and Frank Ernest Hill, *Ford: The Times, the Man, the Company*, (New York: Charles Scribner's Sons, 1954), pp. 89-97.

[10] *New York Times*, December 25, 1921.

[11] Ford Archives, Liebold's Reminiscences, p. 1303; and Richards, *The Last Billionaire*, p. 89.

[12] *Detroit Jewish News*, July 28, 1978.

[13] Burnet Hershey, *The Odyssey of Henry Ford and the Great Peace Ship*, (New York: Taplinger Publishing Co., 1967), p. 18.

[14] Brough, *The Ford Dynasty*, p. 214.

[15] Heywood Broun and George Britt, *Christians Only: A Study in Prejudice*, (New York: Vanguard Press, 1931), pp. 34-39.

[16] Robert Rockaway, in *American Jewish Historical Quarterly*, September 1974.

[17] Nevins and Hill, *Ford: The Times*, p. 46.

[18] Rockaway, *American Jewish Historical Quarterly*.

188

[19] Keith Sward, *The Legend of Henry Ford,* (Toronto: Rinehart and Co., 1948), p. 112.

[20] Charles Herbert Stember, *Jews in the Mind of America,* (New York: Basic Books, 1966), pp. 247-248.

[21] *Detroit Jewish News,* July 28, 1978.

[22] Hershey, *The Odyssey of Henry Ford,* p. 19.

[23] *McClures Magazine,* March 1913

[24] Ibid., January 1907.

[25] *Fortune* magazine, February 1936.

[26] Rockaway, *American Jewish Historical Quarterly.*

[27] *Jewish American,* July 4, 1904.

[28] *Dearborn Independent,* October 2, 1920.

[29] Henry Ford, *Edison: As I Know Him,* (New York: Cosmopolitan Book Corp., 1930), p. 102.

[30] *Detroit News,* October 18, 1931.

[31] Brough, *The Ford Dynasty,* p. 180.

[32] William Adams Simonds, *Edison: His Life, His Work, His Genius,* (New York: Blue Ribbon Books, 1960), p. 312.

[33] Matthew Josephson, *Edison,* (New York: McGraw-Hill Book Company, 1959), p. 457.

[34] Ibid., p. 464.

[35] Sward, *The Legend of Henry Ford,* pp. 113-114.

[36] Ford Archives, Accession Box 64, Edison letter to Bernstein, November 13, 1914.

[37] Ford Archives, Accession Boxes 62/11 and 64.

[38] Harry Bennett, as told to Paul Marcus, *We Never Called Him Henry,* (New York: Fawcett Books, 1951), p. 47.

[39] *Detroit News,* October 18, 1931.

[40] Ford Archives, Accession Box 72, also Box 1; and Liebold papers, Accession 64.

[41] Nevins and Hill, *Ford: Expansion and Challenge,* p. 429.

[42] Michael Sayers and Albert Kahn, *The Plot Against the Peace,* (New York: The Dial Press, 1945), pp. 229-231.

[43] *Friday* magazine, January 24, 1941.

[44] Norman Cohn, *Warrant for Genocide,* (New York: Harper & Row, Publishers, 1966), pp. 160-161.

[45] John Roy Carlson, *Under Cover: My Four Years in the Nazi Underworld of America,* (New York: E. P. Dutton, 1943), pp. 476-477.

⁴⁶ Sward, *Legend of Henry Ford*, p. 94.

⁴⁷ *Friday* magazine, January 24, 1941.

⁴⁸ Spencer Ervin, *Henry Ford vs. Truman H. Newberry*, (New York: Richard R. Smith, 1935), p. 301.

⁴⁹ John S. Rae, *Great Lives Observed: Henry Ford*, (Englewood Cliffs, N.J.: Prentice-Hall, 1969), pp. 163-166.

⁵⁰ Brough, *Ford Dynasty*, p. 106.

⁵¹ *The International Jew*, vol. 1 (Dearborn, Mich.: The Dearborn Publishing Co., 1920), p. 132.

⁵² Merz, *And Then Came Ford*, p. 179.

⁵³ Norman Hapgood in *Hearst's International*, July 1922.

⁵⁴ *Fortune* magazine, February 1936.

⁵⁵ I. Dinnerstein, *The Leo Frank Case*, (New York: Columbia University Press, 1968).

⁵⁶ Saul S. Friedman, *The Incident at Massena: The Blood Libel in America*, (New York: Stein & Day, 1978).

⁵⁷ "Opinions," American Jewish Archives pamphlet, (New York: Carver Printing Co., undated), including statements about Ford's anti-Semitism by Theodore Roosevelt, Col. George Harvey, S. W. Purvis, Arthur Brisbane, Stephen Wise, and Joseph Kranskopf.

Index

•